A MAP OF THE STARS

(SOME OF OUR FAVORITE CUSTOMERS' FAVORITE SPOTS)

DOWNSTAIRS

GLORIA VANDERBILT

BARBRA STREISAND

ANDY WARHOL

DIANA ROSS

PARKER
POSEY

RUDY
GIULIANI

SUSAN
SARANDON

DIANE
SAWYER

DUDLEY
MOORE

DARYL
HANNAH

MIA
FARROW

VANESSA
WILLIAMS

JOAN RIVERS

NICOLE KIDMAN

BROOKE ASTOR

GLENN CLOSE

IVANKA
TRUMP

MELANIE
GRIFFITH

ANTONIO
BANDERAS

BRUCE
WILLIS

SWEET SERENDIPITY

SWEET SERENDIPITY

DELICIOUS DESSERTS
& DEVILISH DISH

STEPHEN BRUCE

WITH BRETT BARA · PHOTOS BY LIZ STEGER

UNIVERSE

CONTENTS

FOREWORD

JOAN: Serendipity 3 has been a New York institution for sixty years! Everybody—and I do mean EVERYBODY—at one time or another ends up at Serendipity for sweet escapes. And now, *Sweet Serendipity—The Diamond Edition* gives you a terrific taste of this legendary restaurant, with dozens of sweet and decadent recipes as well as tasty celebrity tidbits!

The word serendipity means "the art of making happy discoveries—finding the unexpectedly pleasant by chance or sagacity." I first experienced Serendipity in the 1960s. I would meet friends there for lunches, dinners, and post-theater snacks, and we'd treat ourselves to the restaurant's famous "backward meal" (eating dessert *before* you eat your meal) and starting it off with the Frrrozen Hot Chocolate. As the years passed, I started bringing my daughter Melissa there, and now, together, we take my grandson, Cooper. Happily, the tradition continues for three generations.

The warmth of the owner/founder Stephen Bruce is still felt in the restaurant—along with the fun of never knowing who will be seated across from you. Over the years I have munched on foot-long hot dogs while rubbing shoulders with Jackie O, Cher, Andy Warhol, Sarah Jessica Parker, and Mayor Mike Bloomberg, just to name a few.

Serendipity, along with the Empire State Building, Rockefeller Center, and the Central Park Zoo is one of the great New York institutions. I can't wait until Cooper takes his children there. Right, Melissa?

MELISSA: Absolutely right, Mom!

Serendipity plays a large role in my childhood memories of our trips to New York. Every time we would fly in from Los Angeles, one of our first stops would be to go there for the foot-long hot dogs, the Frrrozen Hot Chocolate, and the amazing quirky atmosphere. Now I love bringing Cooper to continue our tradition.

Happy anniversary, Serendipity!

LOVE,
JOAN & MELISSA

The three founding princes of Serendipity, from left: Stephen Bruce, Calvin Holt, and Patch Caradine.

INTRODUCTION

HAPPEN DOWN A SMALL SET OF STAIRS ON A CERTAIN QUIET STREET OF NEW YORK CITY, AND YOU'LL FIND YOURSELF SUDDENLY TRANSPORTED TO A MAGICAL PLACE.

It's a cozy palace where dream-sized desserts and ice cream parlor whimsy lull you into a fantasy of another day and age. It's a grand hideaway where ripples of excitement are touched off every time a tray of luscious fudge-drenched treats passes by. Here you can buy a Tiffany lamp or a teddy bear, dine on a hot dog or caviar, and sit at a table that was once occupied by a Hollywood legend. Andy Warhol, Marilyn Monroe, Jackie Kennedy, and Cary Grant hobnobbed here, and their ghosts seem to linger. Serendipity is a lucky place, unexpected and wonderful, where everyone who walks through the doors is suddenly happier.

It all started in the early 1950s, when three young men, myself among them, found their way to New York City. We were roommates in a humble cold-water flat, and though we each came to the Big Apple to pursue our dreams, one of our main occupations quickly became throwing the most fabulous parties in town. Our soirees were such a hot ticket that it occurred to us that we could turn our love of food, decor, and hosting into a business. And with that, we decided to open a café and gift shop.

It was an unusual idea to say the least. At the time, there was no such thing as a boutique within an eatery. But we were young and carefree and not much bothered with the norm. And so we pooled our resources (a whopping $500), and on September 15, 1954, opened shop in a tiny basement at 234 East 58th Street, on the Upper East Side.

Our trio was made up of Calvin Holt and Patch Caradine, old friends from Little Rock, Arkansas, and myself, Stephen Bruce of New Jersey. Calvin was a soda jerk turned dancer, I was a window dresser and aspiring designer, and Patch was a writer with a serious crossword puzzle obsession.

Patch discovered an intriguing term in the *London Times* crossword puzzle. Invented by eighteenth-century wordsmith Sir Horace Walpole and based on the tale of the three princes of Serendip, it meant "the art of finding the pleasantly unexpected by chance or sagacity." Serendipity! We had found the perfect name. We added a "3" at the end to represent the three of us, the founding princes. At the time, the word was rarely found in dictionaries. Since we began

serendipity 3

234 East 58   N.Y.22   Plaza 3-3963

Announcing the opening of Serendipity 3. Being a General Store for Unexpected Mercantile. Where refreshing ideas in accents for living can be viewed throughout the day ---- the shadow of a real Italian eagle quietly soaring over our 1921 Caffe Espresso chassis. Pressure and steam begin at 5:30 to bring you the best of Exotic blendings in coffees,and old world and South recipes of Ambrossiac goodness. All in Serendipity's setting of purity.

                             Calvin Holt
                             Patch Caradine
                             Stephen Bruce

Now Open
10 A.M. - 12:30 A.M.

Left: Our letterhead, designed by Milton Glaser and Seymour Chwast of Pushpin Studio, and our opening announcement. **Opposite:** Some of the Christmas cards we designed and sent to friends over the years.

using it, "serendipity" has become vogue. And it couldn't have been more ideal: this obscure word summed up our experience in opening a restaurant as well as other people's experience of visiting the place for the first time—we were all discovering something unexpected and wonderful.

MORE FLAIR THAN FINANCE

All we could afford for our new venture was a scant three hundred square feet of basement space, with cracked walls and exposed pipes running along the low ceilings. But we saw its potential, and started by coating everything in bright white paint, envisioning a setting of "pure white purity."

We were determined to fill our space with our personal style—no standard-issue restaurant goods for us. We loved the vintage look of almost-antique furnishings, and we weren't going to let our lack of funds stand in the way. At five cents a ride we journeyed downtown on the Third Avenue elevated train to buy plain, inexpensive dishes at the old china shops on the Bowery. We ventured upstate to find cheap marble-topped tables, bentwood chairs, and discarded old Tiffany lamps. They didn't cost much because nobody liked them

anymore, associating them with the dreary, dark Victorian era. We found two old dining room buffets, painted them white, and used them to display our merchandise. We lined their shelves with an arrangement of organized, stylized clutter: antique feather dusters, vintage toys, outrageous hats, movie posters, voodoo kits, old glassware.

To our delight, we discovered an antique espresso machine in Little Italy. It had seen better days, and seemed in constant danger of exploding, but we were smitten. We loved the idea of serving this exotic European drink to our customers—at the time, espresso was little known and never found outside of Italian restaurants.

Calvin and Patch set our menu, which consisted of regular and chocolate pecan pie, rum cake, and sand tarts. We chose these because, quite frankly, they were all we knew how to make; Patch and Calvin had grown up eating them and had tucked the recipes into their suitcases when they departed for New York. We did invent one concoction of our own: a slushy, chocolatey dessert-drink we called Frrrozen Hot Chocolate. Everything we served was very decadent, very indulgent—and topped with mountains of whipped cream.

CHRISTMAS FROM SERENDI...

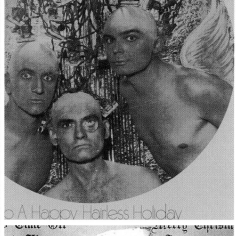

to A Happy Hairless Holiday

to a peripatetic season

Serendipity

I LOVE NEW YORK

TO AN INSTAURATIONAL SEASON

SINGERS

ENDER

Campbell's
CONDENSED

Cream of
Christmas
SOUP

PLAYWIZM

THEATRE DE SERENDIP

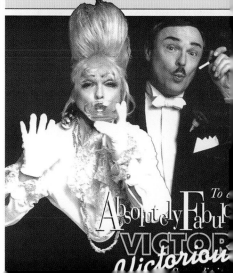

Absolutely Fabu...
VICTOR...

We had more flair than finance, but we made do, baking pies and wrestling with the stubborn espresso maker. We could afford so few dishes that as soon as one customer finished his coffee, we snatched up the cup to wash and reuse for the next person. But somehow our crazy hodgepodge of a café-boutique worked, and in no time it started to catch on.

FOOD AS THEATER

When Serendipity hit the New York restaurant scene, it was unlike anything this city had ever experienced. We served inexpensive, offbeat food in a unique and entertaining setting. We took standard fare and added a twist: an exotic kind of coffee, bipolar "frozen hot" drinks, and naughty, overindulgent sweets—all served up inside a gift shop.

At that time, restaurants consisted of expensive, imposing French eateries or cheap, quick alternatives. New Yorkers who were hungry but not rich could find no-frills sustenance at a soda fountain chain, such as Schrafft's or Childs, or a hot dog from a street vendor. Or they could visit an Automat, a restaurant made up entirely of vending machines. After all, this was the 1950s, and the public was wallowing in an Ozzie and Harriet ideal where everything was predictable and safe. Restaurants were no exception. At just about any establishment, customers would find standard food, standard portions, and standard ambience.

Not so at Serendipity. Just a few months after we opened, a *New York Times* headline read, "Art Shop Has Caffe Espresso." Our coffee was so unusual that it actually made headlines! We gave our customers something to marvel at while they ate—while they also marveled at what they ate. It was food as theater, the opposite of everything else that was happening then, and people loved it. In a one-scoop vanilla world, Serendipity was a giant hot fudge sundae.

The sixties were coming, New York was loosening its tie, and New Yorkers were ready for a new kind of dining experience. Our freewheeling attitude was contagious, and word got out about the best pecan pie anyone had ever tasted—and the wackiest dining room anyone had ever seen. Andy Warhol was one of our first customers, and he used our shop to show his work. In 1956 we were listed in the *New York Times* as the venue for his exhibit described only as "pump pictures." With that, the art crowds flocked in.

We also had the serendipitous fortune of being situated on the same block as some popular restaurants of the day, and the fashionable set seemed to just stumble down our stairs for sweets after dinner. Suddenly (to our delight!) everyone was desserting at Serendipity. Tennessee Williams and Truman Capote were here often. Movie stars, *Vogue* editors, Broadway producers, writers, artists, royalty—they all queued up around the block. One could imagine that after having breakfast at Tiffany's, Holly Golightly might have had lunch at Serendipity!

It quickly became clear that we had indeed discovered something pleasantly unexpected, completely by chance. Serendipity was born.

Opposite: Andy Warhol outside the restaurant and myself in the doorway.
Above: Andy Warhol's effigy hangs over his favorite table.

SERENDIPITY GROWS UP

At all hours of the day and night, a line of very fashionable sugar-seekers spilled out our door. When we first opened, Calvin and Patch made six pies each per week, and by now they were making thirty pies each, a few times per week! We were desperate for more space, so we found a spot just a few blocks away, packed up with a flourish, and moved to our spacious new digs on East 60th Street.

Everything in the new location was the dreariest brown and forest green and in desperate need of our signature touch. We coated every square inch in fresh white paint and had an art deco octagonal tile floor installed. We added fifty more Tiffany lamps and covered every available surface with our unlikely finds: a Pegasus from a Mobil gas station sign, Victorian prints from a Paris hotel that was being razed, street signs, stained glass. At the back of the restaurant we installed a six-foot-tall clock we'd plucked from a neighborhood building facing the wrecking ball. I had started designing hats and clothes, and my creations hung from racks in the gift shop up front. The result felt like some kind of fantasy land. Craig Claiborne wrote in the *Times*, "The dining area resembles a stage set that might have been inspired by the writing of Lewis Carroll. There is an *Alice in Wonderland* effect about the stark white tables, chairs and china, which are surrounded by potted palms, an antique espresso machine and a giant clock similar to those found atop public edifices. A stuffed goose hangs high from a skylight with stained glass panes."

Our magical clock that runs only on Serendipity time.

All we needed was a sign to hang out front, so we called Milton Glaser, the graphic artist who later designed the famous "I ♥ NY" motif, and his partner, Seymour Chwast. Before the days of Serendipity, Calvin had shared a loft on 17th Street with Glaser, a recent fellow Cooper Union graduate. For their pal, Glaser and Chwast created the three princes logo that remains the symbol of Serendipity to this day.

PRESENTATION IS EVERYTHING

Our larger kitchen allowed us to begin serving lunch and dinner. We added simple fare that was at once familiar—hot dogs, ice cream, omelets— but served in a way unlike anything anyone had ever seen: foot long hot dogs, ornate sundaes, omelets with caviar. It was timeless food that tapped into nostalgic cravings, while exciting and new at the same time. We were ahead of our time: In 1990 Florence Fabricant said in the *Times*, "There's nothing unusual about iced cappuccino, green chili omelets, and chocolate pecan pie. Not today. But consider this: they were all on the menu at Serendipity some thirty years ago."

The legendary chef James Beard took us under his wing and taught us to make omelets and chili. Even more scintillating than our expanded menu was the theatrical preparation and presentation: Calvin and Patch could be found most days beating eggs to order at their omelet station at the back of the dining room, both of them decked out in three-piece suits. Even our hot dogs were above par—Calvin and Patch had eaten foot longs in the south, but the lengthy dogs were unknown here in New York, so we had to have them specially made. Our sundaes were the most enormous production of all, evolving into outrageous proportions. They

Jacqueline Kennedy Onassis and John Kennedy Jr. after a visit to Serendipity.

were served in a giant goblet, topped with copious amounts of whipped cream and rivers of hot fudge, all of it spilling over the edges of its dish. "Ooh" and "aah" became the most common sounds heard at Serendipity, echoing throughout the dining room every time a tray passed with one of the huge, spectacular desserts!

All three of us washed dishes, waited tables, cooked, charmed customers, and everything else. What had started out as a lighthearted diversion had become more than a full-time job, and we were loving every minute of it.

Within a few years we hired our first waiters and cooks to help handle the never-ending crowds. Encouraged to cultivate "controlled eccentricity," our staff was attentive, courteous to a fault, and as outrageous as the law would allow. The waiters, who reported for work wearing three-piece suits, did whatever it took to make our customers feel like

stars. One day, three French women came in with their hair dyed chartreuse, orange, and fuchsia, respectively. Their garçon dipped into some Easter egg dyes and coordinated the whipped cream on their sundaes to match their 'dos. One regular customer came in at least three times a week with her three Pekingese, and every time, without fail, each was promptly served a bowl of water with a maraschino cherry. When Jim Henson stopped by in 1979, he was served tea in a Miss Piggy mug. And when George Steinbrenner visited in 1999, our chef carved a pumpkin with the Yankee logo, which was presented to Mr. Steinbrenner at his table. He liked it so much that he gave the entire staff tickets to the World Series in return.

A SERENDIPITOUS ANNIVERSARY

In 1966, the *Times* described Serendipity as having "the peculiar distinction of remaining fashionable longer than most of its customers (12

years)." Luckily, we managed to far surpass that milestone! As the years passed, Serendipity continued to be a hub for the city's most cutting-edge artists, designers, and actors.

The restaurant guide *Frommer's* said of us in 1977, "We doubt if there's another place in New York—or anywhere else, for that matter—quite like Serendipity. The prettiest people lunch and meet here for afternoon tea and after theater. Personally, we have long found Serendipity to be one of the city's happier happenings."

Our style seemed to catch on, and our unorthodox approach to dining set the pace for scores of restaurants to come. Within a few years of our opening, a multitude of themed restaurants, which bore an uncanny resemblance to Serendipity, began popping up. But we'd like to think that none measure up to the original. Why were we so successful, even in the face of so much imitation and competition? "The drug here is ice cream, luscious, fudge-drenched mountains of it, which has the addicting effect of making everyone who eats it very, very happy," the *Daily News* wrote in 2000.

Through the years, we made news at every turn. In the seventies Calvin set a culinary record on television for stuffing an egg into a quail, into a duck, pheasant, goose, and finally into a 29-pound turkey. Later we made waves when we held a séance to make contact with the spirits of Andy Warhol and Marilyn Monroe, and when we married a loyal pair of customers in a bathtub full of Frrrozen Hot Chocolate. We are continually showing up in the *New York Post* every time Nicole Kidman, Jack Nicholson, Meryl Streep, or any other superstar is seen in our dining room.

New York magazine called us one of its 100 favorite restaurants, and *Gourmet* included us on an exclusive list of "Great Chocolate Desserts," adding that at Serendipity "one may drink or eat one's way to chocolate satiety." Our popularity seemed to spread around the globe—the London newspaper *The Independent* listed us as one of the fifty best experiences in New York. The *New York* and *Los Angeles Times* called us a landmark, an institution, the most famous ice cream parlor in New York City.

These are all great honors, to be sure. But I feel even more honored when I see stars like Cher coming back day after day for their favorite dish, or icons like Yoko Ono waiting patiently in line for a table. But perhaps the greatest pleasure of all comes from seeing longtime customers return with their children and grandchildren, making us a part of their family traditions. Or when visitors to New York simply must come to Serendipity to see the place they've heard and read so much about.

It's hard to believe that it's been fifty years since we first opened the doors of our little base-

ment café. Who would have imagined then that what started out as a whim would become our life's work? My two partners have passed on, but we created a legacy that stretches across the seas. I know they would be very proud, as I am, to celebrate our fiftieth anniversary with the publication of this book. I hope you'll enjoy this collection of tales that traces fifty fabulous years of delectable treats, happy accidents, and memorable moments. And I hope you'll enjoy making the recipes that have made us the sweetest restaurant in New York City.

Finally, I hope you'll remember to let life take you where it may. You never know when serendipitous adventures are going to lead to dreams come true—even when they may be dreams you never knew you had.

— S T E P H E N   B R U C E

TREMEND

STUPE

OUS

NDOUS

CAKES

THE MANOR BORN BANANA CAKE

WITH COFFEE BUTTERCREAM

One noble 8-inch three-layer cake for 6 or more

FOR THE CAKE:

Unsalted butter for the pans

2 1/4 cups cake flour

2 teaspoons baking powder

1 teaspoon baking soda

1/4 teaspoon salt

7 tablespoons unsalted butter, softened

1 1/3 cups sugar

1 cup (scant) mashed ripe bananas (about 2 medium)

2 large eggs

scant 1/2 cup buttermilk

1 cup coarsely chopped pecans

FOR THE FROSTING:

6 large egg yolks

1 cup sugar

1/2 cup water

2 cups (4 sticks) unsalted butter, cut into small pieces and softened

2 tablespoons instant espresso powder

1 teaspoon boiling water

• To make the cake: preheat your oven to 375 degrees. Butter three 8-inch round cake pans and line with parchment paper. Sift together the flour, baking powder, baking soda, and salt, and set aside. In a medium mixing bowl, cream the butter and sugar. Add the bananas and mix well. Add the eggs and buttermilk, and mix until fully incorporated. Add the flour mixture, stirring only until incorporated. Fold in the pecans. Spread the batter equally in the three pans, smoothing with a spatula.

• Bake for 8 to 12 minutes, until the cakes are golden brown and spring back when touched. Cool the cakes in their pans for 5 minutes on a rack, then remove them from pans and cool on a rack until they are room temperature.

• While the cakes are cooling, make the frosting: in a medium bowl, beat the yolks with an electric mixture until light in color. In a small, heavy-bottomed saucepan, combine the sugar and 1/2 cup of water and cook over medium heat until the syrup reaches 238 degrees on a candy thermometer.

• With the mixer running on medium speed, pour the hot sugar syrup into the yolks in a very slow stream down the side of the bowl. Continue to beat the yolk and syrup mixture on medium speed until it cools to room temperature.

• Keep the mixer running on medium speed and add the butter gradually, bit by bit, continuing to beat until fully incorporated and fluffy. Meanwhile, mix the espresso powder with the boiling water until fully dissolved; then add it to the finished buttercream and beat until incorporated.

• To assemble the cake, stack all three layers with one-quarter of the frosting between each, and coat the top and sides with the remaining frosting. For extra pomp, you may pipe some of the frosting with a pastry bag along the edges of the cake and garnish with coffee beans. Chill until the frosting is set. Store at room temperature, loosely covered.

MAD KING LUDWIG'S CHOCOLATE CAKE

One royal 8-inch three-layer cake for 6 or more

FOR THE CAKE:

Unsalted butter for the pans

8 ounces semisweet chocolate, coarsely chopped

1/2 cup boiling water

1/2 pound (2 sticks) unsalted butter, softened

2 cups sugar

4 large eggs, separated

1 teaspoon vanilla extract

2 1/2 cups cake flour

1 teaspoon baking soda

1/2 teaspoon salt

1 cup buttermilk

FOR THE FROSTING:

2 cups half-and-half

2 cups sugar

6 large egg yolks

1/2 pound (2 sticks) unsalted butter, cut into 1/2-inch cubes and softened

2 teaspoons vanilla extract

2 2/3 cups flaked, sweetened coconut

2 cups finely chopped pecans

• To make the cake: preheat your oven to 350 degrees and line three 8-inch round cake pans with buttered parchment paper.

• Place the chocolate in a bowl and pour boiling water over it, slowly stirring with a spatula until smooth. Let cool. Cream the butter and sugar on medium-high speed until fluffy, about 3 minutes. Add the egg yolks one at a time, beating well after each addition. Add the vanilla extract and cooled melted chocolate and mix until combined.

• Sift together the flour, baking soda, and salt. At low speed, mix the dry ingredients into the butter mixture alternately with the buttermilk in three additions.

• In a clean bowl with clean beaters, beat the egg whites to stiff peaks. Fold them gently into the batter.

• Scrape the batter evenly into the prepared pans and bake for 30 to 40 minutes, or until a cake tester inserted into the center of the cake comes out clean. Cool the cakes in their pans for 10 minutes. Then invert each cake onto a wire rack and cool completely, right-side up.

• While the cakes are cooling, make the coconut-pecan frosting: in a medium saucepan, heat the half-and-half to a simmer. Meanwhile, in a large bowl, whisk the sugar into the egg yolks. When the half-and-half comes to a boil, pour over yolk mixture, whisking vigorously. Return the mixture to the saucepan and cook over medium heat until thick. Do not allow to boil. Cover the custard tightly with plastic wrap and chill in the refrigerator until room temperature. Cream the butter; add the custard and whip until fully incorporated, then mix in the vanilla, coconut, and pecans.

• To assemble the cake, stack the layers with one quarter of the frosting between each. Cover the top and sides with the rest, and enjoy a dessert fit for a king.

LIZA MAE'S CHOCOLATE ROLL

One creamy 11-inch roll for 6 or more

FOR THE CAKE:

Unsalted butter for the pan

1/2 cup all-purpose flour

1 teaspoon baking powder

3 tablespoons unsweetened cocoa

Pinch of salt

1/2 cup sugar

2 large eggs, separated, room temperature

2 tablespoons water

2 teaspoons vegetable oil

1/4 teaspoon vanilla extract

Confectioners' sugar for dusting

FOR THE SYRUP AND FILLING:

3 tablespoons sugar

1/4 cup water

Splash of your favorite liqueur, such as Kahlúa or kirsch (optional)

1 cup heavy cream

FOR THE FROSTING:

1 cup heavy cream

3 ounces semisweet chocolate, chopped

• To make the cake: preheat your oven to 400 degrees. Generously butter a 12 x 17-inch sheet pan, line it with parchment paper, and butter the parchment paper. Have a second clean sheet pan and piece of parchment ready.

• Sift together the flour, baking powder, cocoa, and salt, and set aside. Slowly beat 1/4 cup of the sugar into the yolks in a medium bowl. Beat on high until light and fluffy, about 1 minute. Add the water, oil, and vanilla, and beat until incorporated.

• In a clean medium bowl with clean beaters, beat the egg whites and remaining 1/4 cup of sugar until stiff peaks form, about 2 minutes. Do not overbeat; the whites should appear glossy but not curdled.

• Using a large spatula, gently fold the whites into the yolks mixture in two parts, stopping when there are still some white streaks. Gently fold the flour mixture into the egg mixture in two parts. Do not overmix; stop as soon as the flour is completely incorporated.

• Spread the batter evenly in the prepared pan using an offset spatula. The batter will form a very thin layer: be on the lookout for areas that are too thin and fill these in. Bake in the top third of the oven for 7 to 10 minutes (the darker your pan, the less time it will take to bake). The cake is done when it is no longer puffy, pulls away from the pan, and springs back when touched.

• Immediately place the baking sheet on a heatproof surface and dust the cake with a generous layer of confectioners' sugar. Cover the cake with the reserved parchment paper and the second sheet pan, right side up. Invert the entire stack in one quick motion. The cake should immediately plop onto the outside bottom of the clean pan; if not, gently tug at a corner of the baked parchment until it does. Peel off the baked parchment (now on top).

• Immediately trim 1/2 inch from all sides of the warm cake using a serrated knife. Allow the cake to cool slightly. Meanwhile, make the syrup by bringing 2 tablespoons of the sugar and 1/4 cup of the water to a full boil. Take off heat and add liqueur, if using. Set aside. Make the whipped cream filling: beat the cream with the remaining 1 tablespoon of sugar until soft peaks form. Set aside at room temperature. Make the frosting: pour the cream into a heavy-bottomed saucepan, preferably nonstick, and bring to a boil over medium heat. Remove from the heat and immediately add the chocolate, stirring slowly with a rubber spatula until fully blended. Cool until lukewarm.

• If you must assemble the cake later, cover and store in fridge. Allow to come to room temperature before proceeding. Final assembly: brush or sprinkle a thin layer of the sugar syrup all over the cake so that it is flexible but not mushy. Spread all of the filling over the cake using an offset spatula. Now it's time to roll it all up. Arrange the cake with one of the short sides toward you. Starting from the far short edge, roll the cake tightly but gently toward you. The cake may crack, but keep going, gently patting it into an even roll shape. Refrigerate the roll, seam side down, for at least an hour.

• Pour and spread the frosting over the roll. If you're feeling artistic, drag a fork through the frosting to create designs. Allow the cake to set at room temperature, but do not refrigerate. It will keep, covered, for up to 3 days at room temperature. To serve, slice crosswise, revealing a spiral of cake and filling.

OH NO, IT'S YOKO ONO

We generally try to treat celebrities like regular customers and discourage overzealous fans. But when Sharon Stone visited us during the filming of *Gloria*, she was attacked by an overzealous fern. The plant latched onto the wig she was wearing as part of her costume, and as Sharon tried to untangle herself it just got worse. Sharon held no grudge.

Sometimes the stars themselves get star struck—Meg Ryan and Dennis Quaid came in with their son, Jack, in 1996. As Meg shopped in the boutique, a fan rushed up to Dennis and excitedly asked, "Is that Meg Ryan?" Dennis, unrecognized, laughed and said, "Yeah, that's her, all right," as they both stared at her in awe. Courtney Love came into Serendipity with Edward Norton and her daughter Frances Bean. After dinner the cashier asked, "Aren't you Courtney Love?" to which Courtney replied, "Who's that?"

Sometimes we don't even notice celebrities. When Bijou Phillips asked for a table, she was told it would be forty-five minutes and she could put her name on the waiting list. "Ono," she said, but the harried maître d' asked, "Well, do you want to put your name on the list or not?" "Ono," she replied. "So you don't want a table?" the maître d' shot back. Luckily, I noticed Bijou's boyfriend Sean Lennon and his mother Yoko Ono in the background and showed them to a table.

CELESTIAL CARROT CAKE

In the psychedelic sixties, Patch and Calvin transformed the upper floor of the restaurant into a hippies-only health food haven called the Zen Hashery. It featured recipes from a cookbook the pair had published, *Brown Rice and Love*. Then, *Vogue* shot a story about Serendipity that promoted the health benefits of carrot juice and brown rice. That was all it took for the crowds to flock to the hashery. John Lennon and Yoko Ono were regulars—they even tried to buy part of the decor, a print that featured a cannabis leaf pattern. We couldn't part with it, but John and Yoko didn't hold it against us. Calvin's carrot cake may not be health food by today's standards, but in the sixties it qualified as good-for-you fare.

One healthy cake for 6

FOR THE CAKE:

1 1/2 cups vegetable oil plus extra for the pans

2 cups sugar

3 large eggs

1 teaspoon vanilla extract

2 1/4 cups all-purpose flour

2 teaspoons baking powder

2 teaspoons ground cinnamon

2 teaspoons ground ginger

1/4 teaspoon ground cloves

1/4 teaspoon ground nutmeg

1 teaspoon salt

1 (6-ounce) can pineapple

2 cups shredded carrots

1 cup dried, unsweetened coconut

1 cup chopped walnuts, plus extra for sprinkling on top

FOR THE FROSTING:

1/4 cup unsalted butter

8 ounces cream cheese

1 teaspoon vanilla extract

4 cups confectioners' sugar

• Preheat your oven to 350 degrees. Grease two 9-inch round cake pans with a little oil and line with parchment paper. In a large bowl, combine the oil, sugar, eggs, and vanilla. Sift together flour, baking powder, spices, and salt, and blend into the oil mixture until well combined. Drain the pineapple, and if it is not crushed already, chop it coarsely. Add the pineapple, carrots, coconut, and walnuts to the batter, and stir to combine. Divide the batter between pans and bake for 50 to 60 minutes, or until a cake tester comes out clean.

• To make the frosting, bring the butter to room temperature, then cream it with the cream cheese and vanilla. With the mixer on low, add the confectioners' sugar and blend.

• Cool cakes on a rack in their pans for 10 minutes. Invert and then reverse the cakes. Cool on the rack until room temperature. Once cakes are completely cool, spread one-quarter of icing between the two layers, then frost top and sides.

"I'LL NEVER FORGET THE FIRST TIME I VISITED SERENDIPITY 3 WITH MY TWINS. THE LOOK ON THEIR FACES WHEN THEY HAD THEIR VERY FIRST FRRROZEN HOT CHOCOLATE REMINDED ME OF THE LOOK ON MY FACE WHEN I HAD MINE. THE APPLE DOES NOT FALL FAR FROM THE TREE, BECAUSE WE ALL LOVE IT."

— MICHAEL STRAHAN

MISSISSIPPI MUD CAKE

One gooey nine-inch round cake for 6 or more

FOR THE CAKE:

2 sticks unsalted butter, softened, plus extra for the pan

1 1/2 cups all-purpose flour, plus extra for the pan

1 1/2 cups alkalized cocoa

2 cups sugar

4 large eggs

1 cup coarsely chopped pecans

1 teaspoon vanilla extract

4 cups marshmallows

FOR THE TOPPING:

1 1/2 cups confectioners' sugar

1/2 cup alkalized cocoa

1 cup chopped pecans

1/2 cup evaporated milk

1/2 pound (2 sticks) butter, melted and cooled

• Preheat your oven to 350 degrees. Butter and flour the bottom and sides of a 9-inch round cake pan.

• Sift together the flour and cocoa. Cream together the butter and sugar until fluffy. Add the eggs one at a time, beating well after each addition. At low speed, mix the dry ingredients into the butter mixture. Add the chopped pecans and the vanilla extract and continue mixing until combined.

• Scrape the mixture into the prepared cake pan and bake on a rack in the middle of the oven for 25 to 30 minutes. Remove the cake and sprinkle the top with the marshmallows, then return it to the oven and continue baking until the marshmallows melt and start to brown. Remove from the oven and let cool in the pan set on a rack.

• To make the chocolate-pecan topping: sift together the confectioners' sugar and the cocoa into a medium bowl. Add the pecans, evaporated milk, and melted butter, and mix until combined. Slice the cake into wedges to serve, and drizzle topping over cake as desired. Store loosely covered at room temperature.

"I CAME TO NEW YORK 57 YEARS AGO AND I DIDN'T KNOW WHAT SERENDIPITY MEANT. I SURE AS HELL DO NOW."

—ELAINE STRITCH

PINEAPPLE LEI CAKE

One hulalicious 10-inch round cake for 8 or more

Unsalted butter for the pan

1 1/2 cups all-purpose flour

3/4 cup sugar

3/4 teaspoon baking powder

1/4 teaspoon baking soda

1/4 teaspoon salt

9 tablespoons (1 stick plus 1 tablespoon) unsalted butter, softened

3 large egg yolks

1/2 cup sour cream

1 teaspoon vanilla extract

1 (20-ounce) can pineapple chunks, well drained (about 2 1/2 cups pineapple)

1/3 cup packed light or dark brown sugar

Confectioners' sugar for dusting

• Preheat your oven to 350 degrees. Butter a 10-inch cake pan, and line it with parchment paper.

• Sift the flour, sugar, baking powder, baking soda, and salt into a large mixing bowl. Add the butter and blend until the mixture has the consistency of peas. Add the yolks, sour cream, and vanilla, and mix only until everything is incorporated.

• Spread the batter evenly in the prepared cake pan. Sprinkle the pineapple over the batter, then the brown sugar over that. Bake for 40 to 50 minutes, until the cake pulls away from the sides of the pan and the sugar is bubbly on top. Immediately run a metal spatula around the sides of the cake to loosen it.

• Allow the cake to cool completely. Invert onto a parchment-covered plate, remove the parchment, then turn back right side up onto a serving plate. Serve warm or at room temperature, sprinkled with confectioners' sugar and cut into wedges. Store tightly wrapped at room temperature.

"I FIRST VISITED THE WONDROUS SERENDIPITY IN *1967*.
I WAS SEVENTEEN YEARS OLD AND IT WAS LIKE
ENTERING A MAGIC WORLD. AND THEN THE DESSERTS!
WHAT CAN I SAY—I'M GLAD I WAS SKINNY!"

— TWIGGY

SUMMERHOUSE CAKE

Marlene Dietrich fell in love with this rich Southern confection and wanted to purchase a whole cake to go—until we told her the price. "Under all that glamour, she's a hausfrau," apologized her escort, *Vogue* editor Leo Lerman. "Forgive her if $4 per pound is too expensive for cake, even if she did just come from buying two $10,000 gowns. She's a very practical woman."

One smashing 9 x 5-inch loaf cake for 6 or more

14 tablespoons (1 3/4 sticks) unsalted butter, softened, plus extra for the pan

1 cup sugar

3 large eggs, separated, room temperature

1 1/2 tablespoons lemon extract

1/4 cup Kentucky bourbon plus extra for soaking

1 3/4 cups all-purpose flour

1 1/2 cups raisins

1 1/2 cups very coarsely-chopped pecans

• Preheat your oven to 325 degrees. Butter a 9 x 5-inch loaf pan and line it with parchment paper.

• In a large mixing bowl using the paddle attachment, cream the butter and sugar until light and fluffy. Add the egg yolks, lemon extract, and 1/4 cup of bourbon, and mix until smooth. Whip the egg whites in a clean medium mixing bowl using the whip attachment until soft peaks form. Gently fold the whites into the butter mixture, stopping when there are still white streaks in the batter.

• Sift the flour onto the batter in three portions, folding carefully each time. Be careful not to overmix; stop while you can still see a bit of flour. Fold in the raisins and pecans until uniformly combined.

• Scrape the batter into the prepared cake pan and smooth the top. Place a shallow pan of hot water on the bottom rack of the oven and place the cake pan in it. Bake for 1 1/2 hours, or until a cake tester inserted in the center of the cake comes out clean.

• Cool the cake in the pan for 20 minutes. Remove the cake from the pan by inverting the pan and removing the parchment paper, then let the cake cool completely, right side up on a wire rack.

• Wrap the cake in a triple layer of cheesecloth, and secure the cheesecloth with cooking twine. Wet the cheesecloth liberally with bourbon, all over the cake. Wrap the cake tightly in a layer of aluminum foil and store in a cool, dry place for at least 24 hours to allow the bourbon to soak in and all the flavors to meld. To serve, cut the twine and fold back the cheesecloth. Cut the cake into slices.

MISS RUBY LAUREEN'S GINGER BREAD

Miss Ruby was Calvin's cousin, and this ginger bread was her specialty.

Two spicy 10-inch square cakes for 12 or more

1 1/4 cups shortening, plus extra for pans

2 1/2 cups plus 1 tablespoon all-purpose flour

2 1/2 cups cake flour

2 teaspoons ground cinnamon

1 1/2 teaspoons each of ground nutmeg and ground allspice

1 tablespoon ginger

3/4 teaspoon each of ground cloves and ground mace

1 1/2 cups sugar

3 large eggs

1 tablespoon baking soda

2 1/4 cups buttermilk

1 1/2 cups molasses

Whipped cream, page 56

• Preheat your oven to 375 degrees. Grease two 10 x 10-inch square cake pans, line with parchment paper, and grease the parchment.

• Sift together the flours and spices and set aside. In the bowl of a mixer with a paddle attachment, cream together the sugar and shortening until fluffy. Add the eggs, one at a time, mixing to incorporate each before adding the next. Dissolve the baking soda in the buttermilk. Add the molasses to the batter, then the buttermilk. On low speed, add the dry ingredients, one cup at a time, until combined. Do not overmix.

• Divide the batter evenly between the prepared pans and place on the center rack of the oven. Bake about 35 minutes, until a cake tester inserted into the center of the cake comes out clean. Cool on a rack for 5 minutes, then turn out of the pans and let cool thoroughly.

• Store tightly wrapped at room temperature. To serve, cut into 3 x 3-inch squares and top with whipped cream. You may dust the tops with confectioners' sugar also if you like.

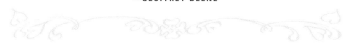

"THERE IS A JOYOUS INDIVIDUALITY ABOUT SERENDIPITY.

THERE'S SOMETHING SO NATURAL ABOUT THE PLACE.

IT EXPRESSES FREEDOM."

—GEOFFREY BEENE

CHOCOLATE BLACKOUT CAKE

When this deep, dark, and dense cake hit the menu, Mia Farrow was smitten and asked for the recipe. The star-struck waiter who fetched it for her forgot to mention that the formula was restaurant-size—enough to make three whole cakes. Mia was apparently up to her elbows in blackout, but who says that's a bad thing? Especially if you have a house full of children.

One pitch-dark 9-inch four-layer cake for 8 or more

FOR THE CAKE:

Unsalted butter for the pans

3 cups cake flour

1 3/4 teaspoons baking soda

1 pound (4 sticks) unsalted butter, softened

2 pounds (about 4 1/2 cups packed) light brown sugar

7 large eggs

2 teaspoons vanilla extract

2 1/2 cups cold water

1 cup sour cream

1 pound unsweetened chocolate, melted and cooled

FOR THE ICING:

1 pound unsweetened chocolate, finely chopped

2 cups heavy cream

2 1/2 cups sugar

1 1/2 tablespoons light corn syrup

1 tablespoon vanilla extract

2 cups sour cream

3/4 cup chocolate chips (semisweet, regular or mini)

• To make the cake, preheat your oven to 325 degrees. Butter the bottoms of four 9-inch round cake pans and line with parchment paper.

• Sift together the flour and baking soda. In a medium bowl, cream the butter and sugar. Add the eggs and vanilla and mix thoroughly. Add the dry ingredients in three parts, alternating with the cold water. Mix completely. Add the sour cream and melted chocolate and mix until incorporated.

• Divide the batter evenly among the prepared pans. Bake for 30 to 40 minutes, until the cakes have puffed and pulled away from the sides of the pans. Cool the cakes in their pans on a rack for 15 minutes. The cakes will sink to half their height—don't worry, that's normal. Remove them from their pans and cool completely on racks.

• To make the icing, place the chopped chocolate in a large mixing bowl. Heat the cream, sugar, and corn syrup in a medium saucepan just to boiling. Pour over the chopped chocolate, then slowly stir until smooth. Add the vanilla and allow to cool completely; then beat in the sour cream. The icing should be glossy.

• To assemble your cake, place one cake layer on a plate. Top it with 1/2 cup of the icing and 1/4 cup of the chocolate chips. Repeat with next two layers. Top the cake with the final layer and cover the entire cake with remaining icing. Store covered at room temperature. Garnish with fresh berries if you like. Any leftover slices can be used to make a Forbidden Broadway Sundae, page 117.

CRÈME DE LA CRÈME CHEESECAKE

One ultimate 10-inch cake for 8 or more

2 cups walnuts, finely chopped

2 tablespoons unsalted butter, softened

4 tablespoon all-purpose flour

2 pounds (four 8-ounce packages) cream cheese

2 cups sugar

2 tablespoons vanilla extract

6 large eggs

4 teaspoons lemon juice

16 ounces (1-pint container) sour cream

• Preheat your oven to 250 degrees.

• Make the crust by blending together the walnuts, butter, and flour in a food processor until smooth. Press into the bottom of a 10-inch springform pan lightly with your fingers.

• Blend the cream cheese and sugar on low speed until smooth. Do not overmix, or air will be incorporated, which will cause the cake to crack. Slowly add vanilla and eggs; mix. Add lemon juice and sour cream; mix just until batter is homogeneous.

• Scrape the batter into springform pan, tapping lightly on counter to allow any air bubbles to rise to the surface. Bake on the middle rack of your oven for 2 hours until all but the center portion (size of a half-dollar) of cake is set. Remove from oven and immediately run a spatula around the edge of the pan to release cake from pan. Allow to cool to room temperature, then refrigerate until firm. Remove springform ring. Store covered in the refrigerator. Garnish slices with fresh berries if you like. If there's any cheesecake leftover, use it to make a Strawberry Fields Sundae, page 118, or a Cheesecake Vesuvius Sundae, page 123.

LET IT SHINE

In the late seventies, our gift shop was stocked with candles in the shape of—ahem—male genitalia. They were a great hit, but pressure from the neighborhood association caused us to pull the candles off the shelves and banish them to the basement. Then came July 13, 1977, the night of the New York City blackout. All five boroughs were left in complete darkness for over 24 hours, and looting, riots, and fires broke out citywide. *Time* magazine called it a "Night of Terror." People cowered in their homes and feared for their lives, and almost every restaurant in the city was dark. Only Serendipity was open for business, basking peacefully in the gentle glow of our penile candles.

GRANDMOTHER HOLT'S ROSE WEDDING CAKE

Calvin's grandmother made this white-on-white cake for family weddings in their small Arkansas town. It would be lovely for any special occasion that calls for an elegant dessert.

One heavenly 3-layer cake or 16 x 4-inch loaf for the whole passel

FOR THE GARNISH:

3 large egg whites, room temperature

Pinch of salt

1 dozen organically grown roses, free of any chemicals, partially closed

5 organically grown rosebuds, free of any chemicals, with stems

2 cups superfine sugar

FOR THE CAKE:

Unsalted butter for the pan

4 cups all-purpose flour, plus extra for the pan

14 large egg whites, room temperature

1 1/2 cups sugar

4 teaspoons rose water

1 cup (2 sticks) unsalted butter, melted and cooled

FOR THE FROSTING:

9 large egg yolks, room temperature

1 1/2 cups sugar

3/4 cup water

3 cups (6 sticks) butter, cut into small pieces and softened

1 1/2 tablespoons rose water

• The day before you make the cake, make the garnish. Beat the egg whites and salt to loosen them. (See note on page 69 about using raw egg whites.) Working one rose at a time, hold each rose or bud by its stem and gently paint it, inside and outside, including all nooks and crannies, with a light coating of egg white. Be on the lookout for globs and blot these away. While each rose is still wet, sprinkle it thoroughly with superfine sugar through a fine sieve.

• Lay the roses on clean paper towels to dry, about 24 hours. When dry, you may remove their stems for arranging. Store at room temperature in an airtight container.

• To make the cake: preheat your oven to 300 degrees. Butter and flour a 10-inch round tube pan or a 16 x 4 x 4-inch loaf pan.

• In a large bowl, stir egg whites to break up. Using a clean large whisk attachment, or a hand mixer with clean beaters, on medium speed, beat the sugar into the egg whites in a slow stream. Continue to beat until the whites hold stiff, glossy peaks.

• Sift the flour into the beaten egg whites in four parts, folding with a spatula after each addition. The batter will look terrible, but keep folding—carefully—until most of the white streaks are gone and the batter resembles goat cheese.

• Add the rose water to the melted butter. Carefully pour half of the butter mixture into the side of the batter near the edge of the bowl. Fold it in. Repeat with the remaining butter mixture, folding in carefully but completely.

• Scrape the batter into the prepared pan and level the top. Bake for 1 hour, or until the cake is lightly golden brown and a cake tester inserted in the center comes out clean.

- Cool the cake in the pan, upside down over wax paper, keeping the pan's rim from touching the countertop, for 30 minutes. Turn the cake right side up, still in the pan, and cool to room temperature.

- While the cake cools, make the frosting: in the bowl of an electric mixer, beat the yolks on medium speed. In a medium heavy-bottomed saucepan, preferably nonstick, bring the sugar and water to a boil and cook until mixture reaches 248 degrees on a candy thermometer. With the mixer running on medium speed, immediately pour the hot sugar syrup in a very slow stream down the side of the bowl into the yolks. Turn the speed to high and beat the yolk mixture until it is room temperature. Add the butter in three portions and beat until fully incorporated and fluffy. Beat in the rose water.

- Final assembly: trim off the rounded top of the cooled cake to level it, and cut the cake horizontally into three even layers. Stack the layers with a thin layer of buttercream in between each. Apply a thin coat of buttercream all over the top and sides of the cake, and refrigerate the cake to set, about a half hour.

- Once set, apply a thicker layer of buttercream to the top and sides of the cake. Use the remaining buttercream, a pastry bag, and assorted tips to decoratively pipe a border around the bottom and top edges of the cake. Arrange the sugared roses decoratively over the top of the cake.

CHOCOLATE IS AN APHRODISIAC

There's just something about our cozy tables nestled into snug nooks, and desserts big enough for sharing, that makes Serendipity the perfect place for romance. JFK Jr. used to arrive here on roller skates to meet then-girlfriend Darryl Hannah, and Cindy Crawford came to Serendipity on a date with an eleven-year-old boy. (His father had won the honor at a charity event.) Countless couples have gotten engaged chez nous, and nervous grooms-to-be have requested that we hide diamond rings in just about every dessert on our menu.

It's no surprise then that more than a few couples have chosen to say "I do" at Serendipity. Many brides have descended our spiral staircase and paraded down a makeshift aisle through the dining room. Among the ministers have been Dr. Ruth, Dr. Joyce Brothers, Robin Byrd, and the Honorable Judge Harold Silverman, who also remarried his wife at Serendipity on the occasion of their fiftieth wedding anniversary. One chocoholic couple tied the knot dressed in chocolate-colored formal wear, and another actually said their vows while standing in a bathtub full of Frrrozen Hot Chocolate! Who could imagine a sweeter way to start a new life together?

WORLD'S LARGEST WEDDING CAKE

On Valentine's Day 2001, Serendipity (with a little help from a New York bakery) decided to whip up a cake for a wedding that was being held in the restaurant that day. It was a simple confection, measuring a mere ten feet tall and weighing just 1,600 pounds! It happened to be the biggest cake in the world, and it earned us a spot in history in the *Guinness Book of World Records*. Afterwards, pieces of cake were distributed to homeless shelters throughout the city. Feeling ambitious? Here's the gigantic recipe:

One record-breaking cake

210 pounds (840 sticks) unsalted butter, plus extra for the pans

210 pounds (480 cups) sugar

90 quarts (150 dozen) large eggs

230 pounds (805 cups) all-purpose flour, plus extra for the pans

300 pounds raisins, currants, cherries, and other dried fruits, chopped

400 pounds marzipan

• Begin by building a wooden platform strong enough to support a ton of cake. Have a forklift nearby to transport the cake from your kitchen to the party. Preheat your oven to 350 degrees. Using an electric mixer, cream the butter and sugar. Add the eggs, beating until combined. Add flour, mixing just until combined. Finally, fold in the chopped dried fruits.

• Butter and flour a series of 18 x 26 x 1-inch sheet pans. Pour in the batter. Bake for 20 to 25 minutes each. The cakes are done when they're golden and a cake tester inserted into the center comes out clean. You may need to bake them in several batches, as there will be at least 200 cakes.

• Final assembly: layer the cakes in multiple tiers, covering each tier in rolled marzipan. Using a ladder, decorate according to your preference, with marzipan flowers and leaves.

"WE'VE HAD TOO MANY BIRTHDAY CELEBRATIONS AT SERENDIPITY 3 TO COUNT. ALL A BLAST IN THEIR OWN RIGHT, BUT NONE CAN TOP OUR 'POST-OPENING-NIGHT' GATHERING OF FAMILY AND FRIENDS AFTER MY DAUGHTER BRYCE MADE HER BROADWAY DEBUT IN THE ROUNDABOUT THEATER COMPANY'S PRODUCTION OF TARTUFFE. THE LEGENDARY FRRROZEN HOT CHOCOLATE TASTED JUST THAT MUCH SWEETER."

—RON HOWARD

MELT-IN-YOUR COOK

-MOUTH

ES

AUNT BUBA'S SAND TARTS

In 1955, Cary Grant and Grace Kelly canoodled over tea and sand tarts at Serendipity when they were in New York for the premiere of *To Catch a Thief*. They had just finished filming the movie on the French Riviera, and rumors were flying that an affair d'amour had developed between the two, although they always insisted they were just friends. They held hands and gazed at each other over their tea, and when they left they were so immersed in conversation that they forgot to pay their tab. No one dared to stop them—chase after Cary Grant for an unpaid check? Never! Even if we did desperately need that $4 at the time. Alas, the two never became more than "just friends." Grace Kelly returned to the Riviera, where she fell in love with Prince Rainier of Monaco. She married him and became a real-life fairy-tale princess, abandoning Hollywood forever.

12 crumbly cookies

**3 cups pecans
(about 3/4 pound)**

1/2 pound (2 sticks) unsalted butter, softened, plus extra for the pans

1/2 cup sugar

1 teaspoon vanilla extract

1 1/2 cups cake flour, sifted

• Process the pecans in a food processor until very fine. Using the paddle attachment of a mixer, cream the butter and sugar in a medium bowl for 5 minutes. Blend in the vanilla. Add the ground pecans and flour and beat 1 minute more. Seal the mixture in a covered container and refrigerate at least 3 hours or overnight. The longer the dough chills, the better the final taste.

• When you're ready to bake, preheat your oven to 350 degrees and butter two cookie sheets. To form the cookies, scoop two large tablespoonfuls of the chilled dough into the palm of your hand. Squeeze the dough until it holds its shape, and form into a log about 3 inches long and 1 inch in diameter. Place the logs on a cookie sheet about 2 inches apart. The tarts will spread a bit while baking.

• Bake for 25 minutes, until the cookies are deep brown and firm to the touch. (The size of the cookies will determine how long they should cook; they may need up to 15 minutes more.) Transfer the cookies to a rack to cool. Store in an airtight container at room temperature for up to three days. Save a few to make a Sand Tart Sundae, page 123.

"ALWAYS LOVED THE FRRROZEN HOT CHOCOLATE WITH THICK WHIPPED CREAM BUT—THEY ALWAYS TOLD THE PRESS."

— BARBRA STREISAND

AUNT BUBA'S MACAROONS

Patch's Aunt Buba was a typical Southern lady who lived a very atypical life. Not only did she divorce her first husband, which was a major sin in the Arkansas delta in those days, but she and her second husband lived right next door to her first husband, and she looked after both of them like one big happy family. Each husband had his favorite version of her recipes, including her famous macaroons—one liked chocolate and the other liked plain. Here, Aunt Buba's first husband's favorite macaroons.

About 18 loving macaroons

2 large egg whites, room temperature

5 tablespoons sugar

1/4 teaspoon almond extract

3/4 cup tightly packed shredded sweetened coconut

Unsalted butter for the pan

• Preheat your oven to 325 degrees. Make sure to use squeaky-clean bowls and beaters so that the egg whites will whip up properly. With an electric mixer, beat the egg whites on medium speed, adding the sugar in a slow stream. Continue beating until the whites hold stiff, glossy peaks. Beat in the almond extract. Gently fold in the coconut with a large spoon or spatula.

• Cover a baking sheet in parchment paper, and spread the parchment with plenty of butter. Drop the batter by teaspoon-sized dollops, 1 inch apart. Bake for 15 to 20 minutes until very lightly browned. Do not overbake: the macaroons should be no darker than light tan.

• Transfer to rack and cool to room temperature before devouring. Store in an airtight container at room temperature.

"SERENDIPITY IS ONE OF THE TRUE FAMILY-FRIENDLY PLACES IN NEW YORK CITY. IT WAS ALWAYS HARD TO DRAG MY KIDS AWAY—AND THAT INCLUDES FRANK!"

—KATHIE LEE GIFFORD

"I WAS INTRODUCED TO SERENDIPITY BY THE CHANTEUSE LENA HORNE, INARGUABLY THE CHICEST (NOT TO MENTION THE MOST BEAUTIFUL) WOMAN ON EARTH. SHE TOOK ME ONE DAY TO A BASEMENT ON EAST 58TH STREET, WHERE FASHIONS HUNG HELTER-SKELTER ON PLAIN PIPE RACKS AMID A DAZZLING JUMBLE OF ... THINGS: MAD HATS, FEATHER BOAS LONGER THAN BOA CONSTRICTORS, ODD OBJETS, ODDER JEWELRY, SOME GLITTERING CREATIONS THAT LOOKED LIKE—WAS IT POSSI-BLE?—TIFFANY LAMPS, STREET SIGNS, STORE SIGNS, WINDUP TOYS FROM ANOTHER ERA—ANOTHER PLANET—PLUS THREE LIVELY PRINCES OF THE MAGIC KINGDOM, STEPHEN, PATCH, AND CALVIN, WHO LOOKED A MITE EXTRATER-RESTRIAL THEMSELVES. FIFTIETH ANNIVERSARY? NOT POSSIBLE! THAT WOULD MAKE US ALL MUCH OLDER THAN WE WERE THEN—AND THANKS TO THE SECRET INGREDIENTS IN CALVIN'S CONFECTIONS (STILL AVAILABLE, AT A SLIGHTLY HIGHER TARIFF, AT SERENDIPITY), WE'RE NOT!"

—JAMES LIPTON

NUTTY NED'S WALNUT BARS

2 dozen wholesome bars

FOR THE CRUST:

2 cups all-purpose flour

Pinch of salt

3/4 cup (1 1/2 sticks) unsalted butter, softened

1/2 cup sugar

2 large egg yolks

FOR THE FILLING:

2 cups (4 sticks) unsalted butter

1/2 cup honey

1/2 cup sugar

2 cups packed light brown sugar

8 cups chopped walnuts (about 2 1/3 pounds)

1/2 cup heavy cream

• To make the crust: preheat your oven to 350 degrees. Sift the flour and salt together. With a mixer, cream together the butter and sugar. Beat in the egg yolks. Add the flour mixture, and mix until combined. Press into a 9 x 13-inch pan, and bake for 15 minutes.

• While the crust bakes, make the filling: combine the butter, honey, sugar, and brown sugar in a large saucepan. Bring to a boil and continue to boil for 3 minutes. Remove from heat and stir in the walnuts and cream. Spread the walnut mixture onto the baked crust and return the pan to the oven for another 30 minutes. Cool on a rack until room temperature.

• When cool, slice into 1 x 1-inch bars. For dessert lovers, slice into 3 x 3-inch bars. Store cut bars in an airtight container at room temperature or store while in covered pan at room temperature.

"THE TWO THINGS MOST NEEDED IN LIFE ARE SUGAR AND SEX/ SO PASS THE FRRROZEN HOT CHOCOLATE AND EXTRA WHIPPED CREAM, PLEASE. THAT'S MY FAVORITE/"

—ROBIN BYRD

ORANGE RAISIN COOKIES

Unsalted butter for the pan

2 1/4 cups all-purpose flour

3/4 teaspoon salt

1 teaspoon baking powder

1 cup (2 sticks) unsalted butter, softened

1 1/2 cups sugar

3 large eggs

1 teaspoon vanilla extract

1 3/4 cups golden raisins

3 tablespoons grated orange zest (from 2 to 3 medium oranges)

• Preheat your oven to 375 degrees. Generously butter a cookie sheet. Sift together the flour, salt, and baking powder and set aside. With an electric mixer, cream together the butter and sugar, then add the eggs and vanilla. Add the flour mixture and mix until just blended. Stir in the raisins and orange zest.

• Drop by the tablespoonful onto the buttered cookie sheet, 1 inch apart, and bake for 10 to 12 minutes, until golden. Cool on a rack. Store in an airtight container at room temperature.

A RARE BIRD

One morning we were setting up for the lunch rush when a quiet woman wandered into the gift shop and asked, "How much is dot candlestick in da vindow?" We knew right away that it was Greta Garbo, the notoriously reclusive actress. She had shunned Hollywood some 30 years earlier after completing her last movie, *Two-Faced Woman*, and moved to New York where she lived just a few blocks from Serendipity, on East 52nd Street. She was famous for avoiding any public attention and was rarely seen by anyone. We spent about ten minutes quietly observing her as she browsed—longer than anyone in New York had spent with her in years—when a waiter noticed her and screamed, "It's Garbo!" In the blink of an eye, she flew away, and we never saw her again.

LEMON RAIN DROPS

5 dozen dainty drops

Unsalted butter for the pans

2 cups all-purpose flour

1 tablespoon baking powder

3/4 teaspoon salt

2 medium lemons

Cold water

1/2 cup (1 stick) unsalted butter, softened

1 cup sugar

1 large egg

• Preheat your oven to 300 degrees. Butter two cookie sheets. Sift together the flour, baking powder, and salt. Zest the two lemons into a large mixing bowl, then juice the lemons into a measuring cup. Add enough cold water to the juice to make a scant 1/2 cup liquid, if necessary, and set aside.

• Add the butter and sugar to the zest in the mixing bowl, and cream until fully blended. Add the egg and lemon juice and beat well. Add the dry ingredients and mix only until they are fully incorporated.

• Drop the batter by level tablespoons 2 inches apart onto the prepared cookie sheets. Bake for 10 minutes, until cookies are slightly firm but not browned.

• Transfer the cookies to a rack to cool completely. Do not stack or store until cool. Store in an airtight container at room temperature.

"ON ONE OCCASION I CAME IN WITH 'GREEN SLIME' IN MY POCKET (YOU KNOW, THE YUCKY KID STUFF). I PROCEEDED TO CALL THE WAITER OVER, PRETEND TO SNEEZE INTO MY HAND (FULL OF SLIME), AND ASK IF HE COULD HELP ME CLEAN UP. THE PEOPLE SITTING AROUND ME WERE IN ON THE JOKE. WE ALL HAD A GOOD LAUGH, I'M AFRAID AT THE EXPENSE OF OUR FRIENDLY WAITER."

—GENE SIMMONS, WHO VISITED WITH HIS WIFE, KIDS, AND COLLECTION OF LIVE FROGS—
IN LEATHER CARRYING CASES, OF COURSE.

GODDESS DIANE'S CHOCOLATE CHIP COOKIES

18 celestial 3-inch cookies

2 cups plus 2 tablespoons all-purpose flour

1/2 teaspoon salt

1/2 teaspoon baking soda

12 tablespoons (1 1/2 sticks) unsalted butter, melted and cooled

1 cup brown sugar

1 1/2 cups sugar

1 large egg plus 1 large egg yolk

2 teaspoons vanilla extract

1 to 2 cups of your favorite kind of chocolate chips

1 cup flaked, sweetened coconut

1 cup almond slivers

• Preheat your oven to 325 degrees. Sift the flour, salt, and baking soda together in a medium bowl. By hand or with a mixer in another bowl, cream the butter and sugars until fluffy. Add the egg, yolk, and vanilla and mix completely. Add dry ingredients and blend just until combined, then stir in chips, coconut, and almonds.

• Form 1/4 cup of the dough into a ball. Using your fingertips, pull the ball into two equal halves. Rotate the semicircular halves and rejoin them at their rounded bases, jagged surfaces exposed, again forming a single cookie. Be careful not to smooth the dough's uneven surface. Place the formed dough onto parchment paper–lined cookie sheets, keeping the jagged edges on top to give the cookie more texture. Leave plenty of space between each cookie, as they will spread as they bake.

• Bake, reversing sheets' positions halfway through, until light golden brown edges start to harden yet centers are still puffy. Allow to cool on a rack. Store in an airtight container at room temperature.

"IN A WORLD THREATENED WITH WAR,
I SAY IF EVERYONE HAD A FRRROZEN HOT CHOCOLATE
THEY WOULD CALM DOWN AND GET ALONG BETTER."

— SYLVIA MILES

PATCH'S BOURBON BALLS

This was one of Patch's cherished recipes. He loved making them, especially at Christmas time. He would snack on them as he worked crossword puzzles, his favorite pastime.

Makes 36 tipsy balls

1/2 cup chopped raisins

1/4 cup bourbon

1 cup finely chopped pecans

2 cups chocolate wafer crumbs (about 38 cookies)

1/2 cup packed brown sugar

1/4 cup unsulfured molasses

1/2 teaspoon ground cinnamon

1/2 teaspoon ground ginger

1/4 teaspoon ground cloves

• In a large bowl, drench the raisins with the bourbon and allow to macerate for 15 minutes. Add 1/4 cup of the pecans and all remaining ingredients, and mix well.

• Form the mixture into 1-inch balls and roll the balls in the remaining chopped pecans. Store them in an airtight container in a cool, dark place for at least one week before serving, to allow the flavors to meld.

EVERYBODY WANTS A PIECE

Plenty of customers lust after our sweet treats—but some seem to crave the very restaurant itself. Andy Warhol was such a fan of our look that he asked me to decorate his apartment at 34th Street and Lexington Avenue. I did it up in real Serendipity style: all in white, with one of our prized Tiffany lamps over the dining nook. The Tiffany was only on loan; he returned it five years later when he moved to a new apartment, and it still hangs in the restaurant above one of our best tables. Elizabeth Taylor wanted that same lamp for the set of her 1973 film *Night Watch*. We refused to sell it to her despite her many efforts, so she did the next best thing: an artist visited Serendipity and sketched the lamp, then reproduced it in plastic for the film set. Rod Stewart offered $42,000 for the famous shade and was turned down. Barbra Streisand even tried to buy our floor! In the early sixties, before she made her first film, she came in for a late dinner and announced that she loved our art deco octagonal tile floor and wanted one just like it in her new apartment. She wrote a $25 check as a down payment—enough to buy exactly one square foot. Alas, she never followed through with her decorating plans, but to this day we still have her check.

WORLD-
PIES

FAMOUS

SERENDIPITY'S SUPER-FLAKY PIE CRUST

A single crust for a 9-inch pie

1 tablespoon sugar (optional)

Pinch of salt

1 cup all-purpose flour, plus extra for rolling

1/3 cup (5 tablespoons plus 1 teaspoon) butter, cold, cut into small slices

1/4 cup cold water

• Stir the sugar (if using) and salt into flour. Add half of the butter and cut it into the flour with a pastry cutter or a fork. Add remaining butter and continue to cut until the butter is in pea-sized pieces. Do not overmix, or the dough will be tough, not flaky. Add the water in small amounts, stirring with a fork, until the dough just holds together. Form the dough into a ball, then flatten it into a disk. Wrap in plastic wrap and chill for at least 1 hour.

• Unwrap the chilled dough, dust with flour, and roll out on a well-floured board until it is about 1/8-inch thick. Transfer it to a 9-inch pie pan and trim edges. Chill again, covered, before filling or baking.

• To bake the crust unfilled, preheat your oven to 425 degrees. Line the chilled crust with parchment paper and fill it with dried beans or pie weights. Bake for 10 to 12 minutes; remove the parchment and weights and bake 5 minutes more or until golden.

• Cool to room temperature and use as soon as possible. If you must store, cover tightly and keep at room temperature.

WHIPPED CREAM

Two to 2 1/2 cups, enough for 1 to 8 persons, depending on if you feel like sharing

1 cup heavy cream, very cold

1 teaspoon vanilla extract

1 1/2 tablespoons light corn syrup

• Combine the cream and vanilla and mix well. With an electric mixer with a whisk attachment, start whipping the cream on medium speed. Add the corn syrup slowly while beating. Whip until the cream holds soft peaks.

• Slather, drop, and dollop onto whatever your heart desires.

HUMBLE PIE

One modest 9-inch pie for 6 or more

FOR THE CRUST:

1 1/2 cups (6 ounces) graham cracker crumbs (10 to 12 full-size crackers)

2 tablespoons creamy peanut butter

2 teaspoons unsweetened cocoa powder

6 tablespoons (3/4 stick) unsalted butter, melted and cooled

FOR THE PIE:

6 ounces cream cheese

2 1/2 cups creamy peanut butter

1 1/2 cups sugar

1 teaspoon vanilla extract

1 cup unsalted roasted peanuts, chopped

1 3/4 cups heavy cream

• To make the crust, preheat your oven to 300 degrees. In a medium bowl, blend together the crumbs, peanut butter, cocoa, and melted butter, using a handheld mixer. Scrape the mixture into a 9-inch pie pan. Using your fingers or the back of a spoon, press the mixture firmly onto the base and up the sides of the pan, forming a uniform crust about 1/4-inch thick. Bake for 7 minutes, then cool completely on a rack.

• To make the filling, beat the cream cheese, peanut butter, sugar, and vanilla in a medium bowl with a handheld mixer until smooth. Fold in the peanuts. In a clean medium bowl, using clean beaters, whip the cream to stiff peaks. Carefully fold the whipped cream into the peanut mixture in three additions, until the mixture is a uniform color and no streaks remain.

• Scrape the filling into the cooled crust. Smooth the filling, forming a slight dome in the center. Refrigerate the pie, uncovered, at least one hour. Once the filling has set, cover pie with plastic wrap and chill completely, at least another hour. Serve wedges cold. Store covered in refrigerator. Use any leftover slices to make a Can't Say No Sundae, page 125.

"IT'S LIKE A CARNIVAL EVERY TIME YOU WALK IN. THE MENU, THE FOOD, THE DESSERTS, AND THE CLEVER GEWGAWS! THIS IS NEW YORK AT ITS GREATEST—LONG LIVE PRINCE STEPHEN BRUCE, THE 'S' IN SERENDIPITOUS SCALLA WALLA BALLY-OSIS!"

— MARIO BUATTA

PECAN PIE

One nutty 9-inch pie for
6 or more

4 large eggs

1 cup sugar

1 cup light corn syrup

**2 cups pecan halves (about
1/2 pound)**

1 unbaked pie crust, page 56

**1 large egg yolk,
very lightly beaten**

• Preheat your oven to 375 degrees. In a medium mixing bowl, whisk the 4 eggs to loosen them. Add the sugar and corn syrup and whisk until blended. Stir in all of the pecans; or, stir in two-thirds, reserving the best-looking pieces.

• Pour the pecan mixture into the crust. Decoratively arrange the remaining pecans, if any, over the top of the pie. Bake for 40 minutes, then remove from the oven. (Be very careful, the filling will be liquid and very hot.) Brush the egg yolk over entire surface and return to oven for 30 minutes more. Remove from the oven (the filling will still be liquid) and cool on a rack for 1 hour.

• Refrigerate or store at room temperature until completely set, at least 4 hours. Slice into eight wedges. Store at room temperature.

"WHEN I WAS A YOUNG GIRL, MY MOM AND I LIVED ON THE
UPPER EAST SIDE. ON VERY SPECIAL OCCASIONS, WE WOULD
BOTH GET DRESSED UP: I REMEMBER MOM IN A BLACK-AND-WHITE
HOUNDSTOOTH SKIRT SUIT, AND I WORE OPAQUE WHITE STOCKINGS,
MARY-JANES, AND THAT ITCHY LACE! WE WOULD HEAD
FOR SERENDIPITY FOR THE LARGEST SUNDAE AROUND . . .
COFFEE ICE CREAM, HOT FUDGE, WHIPPED CREAM, AND, MOST
IMPORTANTLY, TWO SPOONS! TO THIS DAY, WHENEVER I THINK OF
SERENDIPITY, I SMILE AT THE MEMORIES OF MY MOM."

— EMME

LEMON ICE BOX PIE

One of the first cooks hired at Serendipity was the fabulous Miss Essie Vaughn, who created our legendary Lemon Ice Box Pie. In the early sixties a condensed milk company was offering a kolinsky fur in exchange for a thousand condensed milk labels, and it just so happened that Miss Essie's new pie recipe called for that very product. Miss Essie piled on the whipped cream, making sure her lemon pie was a big seller. Five hundred pies later, she strolled into the restaurant swathed in her fur.

One deluxe 9-inch pie for 6 or more

FOR THE CRUST:

1 1/2 cups (6 ounces) graham cracker crumbs (10 to 12 full-size crackers)

2 tablespoons ground cinnamon

1/4 pound (1 stick) unsalted butter, melted and cooled

FOR THE FILLING:

2 (14-ounce) cans sweetened condensed milk

4 large egg yolks

1/2 cup lemon juice

Whipped cream, page 56

• To make the crust: In a medium bowl, blend together the crumbs, cinnamon, and butter using a handheld mixer until fully incorporated. Scrape the mixture into a 9-inch pie pan. Using your fingers or the back of a spoon, press the mixture firmly onto the base and up the sides of the pan, forming a uniform crust about 1/4-inch thick. Refrigerate until ready to use.

• To make the filling: In a medium saucepan, preferably nonstick, whisk together the milk, egg yolks, and lemon juice until smooth. Cook the custard over medium heat until very hot to the touch, about 10 minutes, stirring occasionally with a wooden spoon. Do not allow to boil.

• Strain the custard through a sieve into the prepared pie shell. Smooth the filling, forming a slight dome in the center. Refrigerate uncovered at least 1 hour, or until set. Cover with plastic wrap and chill completely, at least another hour.

• Serve wedges cold with plenty of whipped cream, just like Miss Essie did. Store covered in the refrigerator.

"I USED TO LOVE COMING TO SERENDIPITY WITH ANDY WARHOL—
WE WOULD HAVE THE MOST FABULOUS PARTIES THERE.
THEN LATER I'D COME IN WITH MY SON AND WE'D EAT ICE CREAM
FOR DINNER! IT WAS WONDERFUL. WHO WOULDN'T LOVE IT?"

—BABY JANE HOLZER

WARHOL'S SWEET TOOTH

One of our first customers was a shy young man with a portfolio tucked under his arm, strange hair, and enormous eyeglasses. He was an eccentric artist who made his living drawing shoes for ads, and when he was low on cash he paid his tabs with his rejected ad work. These drawings were charming, so we'd frame them and sell them in the gift shop for $25 apiece.

Andy Warhol spent many hours at our tables, making sketches of his friends. He did a series of line drawings of me, portraying me with hearts floating about my head—those twenty-one sketches remain among my most prized possessions. Andy loved to observe people, and when he wasn't drawing he'd sit alone at a table with a copy of the *National Enquirer* with a hole cut in it propped up in front of him, so that he could peek at other customers while pretending to read.

Then that shy artist became famous almost overnight for his pop art paintings of ordinary objects such as Campbell's soup cans and celebrities including Marilyn Monroe. Andy and his entourage would come here between sessions at the Factory, the loft where they hung out and made art, and after nights out at the legendary disco Studio 54. They often threw parties at Serendipity, when the restaurant would be packed elbow-to-elbow with the most exciting and avant-garde crowd.

Once Andy started publishing *Interview* magazine in the seventies, he would come in every month with a stack of the current issue, drop one at every table, and walk quickly out. People would look after him, whispering, "Was that Warhol?"

In his diaries he wrote often of coming to Serendipity with friends. In one entry, he described a night out with Mary Tyler Moore: "She got a craving for a hot fudge sundae so I said Serendipity was the best really good place and she liked the idea of that. When we walked into Serendipity the whole place hushed—'There's Mary.' We sat down under the lamp that was in my living room thirty-five years ago. I ordered half a sundae and so did Mary."

Andy continued to visit Serendipity regularly for his favorite desserts until the time of his death in the late eighties. He had a great yen for sweets and practically lived on Lemon Ice Box Pie.

BIG APPLE PIE

FOR THE CRUST:

8 tablespoons (1 stick) unsalted butter, cold, cut into small cubes

1 cup all-purpose flour, plus extra for dusting

1 cup grated cheddar cheese

3/4 cup cold water

FOR THE FILLING:

1 large egg, separated

5 large Red Delicious or Jonathan Gold apples, peeled, cored, and cut into large chunks

1 cinnamon stick

2 cups apple juice

1 tablespoon vanilla extract

2 tablespoons cake flour

1/3 cup sugar

1 cup sour cream

FOR THE TOPPING:

1/2 pound (2 sticks) unsalted butter, softened

1 cup packed dark brown sugar

2 cups walnut halves

1/2 cup cake flour

2 tablespoons ground cinnamon

• To make the crust: have two identical 9-inch pie pans ready. Add the butter and flour to the bowl of a food processor. Pulse until the mixture has the texture of cornmeal. Add the cheddar cheese and process briefly to blend. With the machine running, pour in the cold water in a steady stream. Process just long enough to completely blend. The mixture will have the texture of cake batter, not a traditional flaky pie crust.

• Scrape two-thirds of the batter into one pie pan. Using your fingers or the back of a spoon, press the mixture firmly onto the base and up the sides of the pan, forming a uniform crust about 1/4-inch thick. Place the remaining batter in a small bowl. Refrigerate both until firm, about 1 hour.

• Remove the firmed crust and remaining batter from the refrigerator. Keeping your hands generously dusted with flour, take small bits of batter from the bowl and mold a rim atop the pie pan edge, taking care to completely join the rim with the main crust. (The rim will prevent this very soft dough from sinking during baking.) Work quickly, as the batter can get soft; if it does, simply refrigerate it again.

• Place the entire crust in the refrigerator to firm again. Meanwhile, preheat your oven to 350 degrees. Once the crust is firm, line it with parchment paper. Set the second pie pan on top of the parchment, so that the two pans are stacked. Fill the top pan with pie weights.

• Bake for 30 minutes, or until crust is partially baked and lightly golden. Remove the upper pan and parchment paper, and cool the crust completely on a rack. You may store the crust at this point, wrapped in plastic.

• To make the filling: preheat your oven to 350 degrees. Brush the egg yolk over the entire rim of the partially-baked pie crust. In a medium saucepan, combine the apples, cinnamon stick, and juice. Cover and bring to a boil. Immediately remove from the heat and drain, reserving the juice for another use (if desired).

• In a large mixing bowl, combine the egg white with the vanilla, cake flour, sugar, and sour cream, and whisk to blend. Add the drained apples and mix to coat completely. Transfer the apples to the shell with a slotted spoon. Pour in as much of the liquid as will fit; you may not need it all.

• Bake 25 to 30 minutes, until the liquid has mostly firmed up.

• Meanwhile, make the topping: in a large bowl, cream the butter and brown sugar with a handheld mixer until light. Add the walnuts and blend. Add the flour and cinnamon and beat 30 seconds more. Refrigerate until needed.

• Remove pie from oven and cover with topping. You may not need all of the topping. Bake for another 15 to 20 minutes, until the topping is browned. Transfer to a rack and cool completely; serve at room temperature. Leftovers are delicious in the Cinnamon Fun Sundae, page 123.

"IN 1976, I STOPPED IN NEW YORK CITY ON
MY WAY HOME FROM ENGLAND, WHERE I HAD JUST FINISHED
SHOOTING STAR WARS. THE SHOOT HAD BEEN DIFFICULT
AND I WAS A BIT DEPRESSED. BRIAN DE PALMA AND STEVEN
SPIELBERG WERE IN NEW YORK, SO WE DECIDED TO GET TOGETHER
AND GO TO SERENDIPITY. I ORDERED NOT ONE FRRROZEN HOT
CHOCOLATE, BUT TWO! MY MOOD IMPROVED IMMEASURABLY."

— GEORGE LUCAS

DEEP-SOUTH BLACK-BOTTOM PIE

One extravagant 8-inch pie
for 6 or more

FOR THE CRUST:

22 small gingersnap cookies

**6 tablespoons (3/4 stick)
unsalted butter, melted and
cooled**

Unsalted butter for the pan

FOR THE CHOCO-
LATE LAYER:

**1 tablespoon (1 envelope)
unflavored powdered gelatin**

3 tablespoons cold water

1 1/3 cups milk

3 large egg yolks

1/3 cup sugar

2 1/4 teaspoons cornstarch

Pinch of salt

**1 1/2 squares (1 1/2 ounces)
unsweetened chocolate**

3/4 teaspoon vanilla extract

FOR THE RUM
LAYER:

3 large egg whites

Pinch of cream of tartar

1/4 cup sugar

2 1/2 teaspoons white rum

Whipped cream, page 56

Shaved chocolate

• To make the crust: place the gingersnaps in a food processor fitted with a metal blade and process until they are fine crumbs. You should have about 1 cup. Add the melted butter, and pulse. With your fingertips or the back of a tablespoon, press the mixture into the bottom and sides of a buttered 8-inch pie pan. Chill in the refrigerator for 30 to 45 minutes.

• To make the chocolate layer: in a small bowl, dissolve the gelatin in the cold water. Set aside. Bring the milk to a simmer in a double boiler. In a medium bowl, beat the egg yolks slightly; combine the sugar, cornstarch, and salt, and stir into the egg yolks. Whisk in the hot milk vigorously.

• Return the mixture to the double boiler; cook, stirring, over hot, not boiling, water, until the custard coats a spoon. Remove from the heat and strain. Stir in gelatin until dissolved. Set aside.

• Melt chocolate in a medium saucepan over very low heat. Remove from heat and slowly stir in the vanilla and one-half of the custard. Beat smooth with a whisk. Cool and pour into the chilled crust.

• To make the rum layer: in a medium bowl, beat the egg whites with the cream of tartar until frothy. Gradually add the sugar and beat until stiff. Carefully fold in the remaining half of the custard and the white rum. Pour as much of this on top of the chocolate layer as it will hold. Reserve the remaining egg whites mixture. Chill the pie for 15 to 20 minutes and pour on the remainder of the egg white mixture. Chill until firm. Serve with whipped cream sprinkled with shaved chocolate.

AUNT LUCILLE'S GEORGIA CHESS PIE

One gorgeous 9-inch pie for 6 or more

1 unbaked pie crust, page 56

1/2 cup (1 stick) unsalted butter

2 ounces (2 squares) bitter-sweet chocolate, chopped

1 cup sugar

2 large eggs, lightly beaten

1 cup pecans, chopped

1 teaspoon vanilla extract

1 tablespoon brandy

- Prepare a 9-inch pie crust, but don't bake.

- Preheat your oven to 325 degrees.

- In a small pot, melt the butter and chocolate together. In a mixing bowl, add the chocolate mixture to the sugar and blend. Add the eggs and blend; add the nuts, vanilla, and brandy, and blend some more.

- Pour this mixture into the pie crust and bake for 30 to 35 minutes, until the edges of the filling puff and begin to crack, and the center is set.

- Cool on a rack to room temperature. Cut in wedges to serve. Cover and store in refrigerator.

"ONCE WHEN I WAS VERY SICK, BEFORE THEY HAD FRRROZEN HOT CHOCOLATE TO MAKE AT HOME, THE PEOPLE AT SERENDIPITY CUT OFF THE TOP OF A MILK CARTON, FILLED IT WITH FRRROZEN HOT CHOCOLATE, WRAPPED IT IN ALUMINUM FOIL, AND SENT IT OUT TO ME. I MUST SAY SOME OF THE MOST SILLY, FUN TIMES I CAN REMEMBER WERE HAD RIGHT UNDER THE HANGING LAMPS."

—CHER

SCHRAFFT'S TUTTI FRUTTI CHIFFON PIE

One fluffy 9-inch pie for 6 or more

1 baked pie crust, page 56

2 teaspoons (2/3 envelope) unflavored powdered gelatin

1 cup plus 1 tablespoon cold milk

1/2 cup heavy cream

6 tablespoons sugar

Pinch of salt

3 large eggs, separated, room temperature

1 tablespoon dark rum

2 tablespoons chopped dried cherries

2 tablespoons chopped dates

2 tablespoons chopped almonds

2 tablespoons chopped candied citrus peel, optional

Whipped cream

Note: This dish uses raw egg whites. The American Egg Board warns against eating uncooked eggs. Although egg whites aren't nearly as likely to harbor bacteria as yolks are, they aren't risk free. Meringue powder, available in baking shops and gourmet and grocery stores, is recommended as a substitute.

• Prepare and bake a 9-inch pie crust as directed until golden brown. Set aside to cool.

• Dissolve the gelatin in 2 tablespoons of the cold milk and set aside. Bring the remaining milk and cream to a boil in a medium saucepan, preferably nonstick, over medium-high heat.

• Meanwhile, in a medium bowl whisk 3 tablespoons of the sugar and the salt into the egg yolks. When the milk mixture is ready, pour it into the yolk mixture, whisking until incorporated. Return the yolk mixture to the pan.

• Over low heat, stirring constantly with a spatula (get into the corners of the pan and scrape the bottom), cook the custard until it thickens slightly, about 2 to 3 minutes. Do not allow it to boil. Remove from heat. Add the gelatin and rum to the warm custard, stirring until completely dissolved. Strain the custard into a medium bowl.

• Cover the custard with plastic wrap, pressing the wrap right onto the surface. Refrigerate until it begins to set (it will be slightly firm to the touch), about 1 hour.

• When the custard is set, in a clean medium bowl with clean beaters, beat the egg whites until fluffy. Slowly add the remaining 3 tablespoons of sugar and beat until stiff peaks form, about 2 minutes. Do not overbeat; the whites should appear glossy but not curdled.

• Add the chopped fruit and nuts to the custard and stir until the custard is broken up. Fold in the beaten egg whites. Do not overmix; stop as soon as there are no more white streaks.

• Pour the custard into baked pie shell, mounding in the center and smoothing to the edges. Refrigerate until completely set (about 4 to 6 hours). Serve chilled, topped with whipped cream, or with more dried fruit and nuts. Store covered in the refrigerator.

THE GREAT PUMPKIN PIE

One awe-inspiring 9-inch pie for 6 or more

1 (15-ounce) can pumpkin puree

3 tablespoons sugar

1 teaspoon ground cinnamon

1/2 teaspoon nutmeg

1/4 teaspoon ground cloves

1/2 teaspoon ground ginger

1/2 teaspoon salt

1/3 cup unsulphured molasses

1 cup milk

3 large eggs

1 unbaked pie crust, page 56

Whipped cream, page 56

• Preheat your oven to 425 degrees. Mix the pumpkin, sugar, spices, and salt in a large bowl. Add the molasses, milk, and eggs and beat until fully incorporated.

• Pour the mixture into the pie crust. Bake for 45 minutes, or until the custard is slightly firm. Allow the pie to cool to room temperature before slicing.

• Store covered at room temperature. Serve wedges with whipped cream.

"'YOU'LL NEVER BE RICH, BUT YOU'LL ALWAYS HAVE NICE
THINGS,' A FORTUNE TELLER ONCE TOLD ME.
THE FIFTY YEARS OF SERENDIPITY HAVE
PROVIDED ME A LIFETIME OF THEM."

— ELEANOR LAMBERT

NOTHING BUT CHANEL NO. 5

After filming *The Seven-Year Itch* in 1955 and divorcing baseball legend Joe DiMaggio, Marilyn Monroe decided to take acting lessons. She wanted to be seen as a serious performer and not just a blonde bombshell, so she came to New York City to study at The Actors Studio.

Marilyn first came into Serendipity with her acting coach, Paula Strasberg, and from then on she would visit us often. She usually came in late in the afternoon wearing a scarf over her head, no makeup, and a trench coat. She was very friendly and down to earth—nothing like the ultra-glamorous Hollywood image the public saw. She'd always ask me to join her for lunch, and on one occasion I could see that beneath her overcoat she had nothing on—except Chanel No. 5, of course!

Late one evening she called and asked if a certain dress was still available in the shop. I told her we still had it, but that it was two sizes too small for her. "That's perfect!" she replied. "I'll be right over." Marilyn arrived shortly, explaining that she was already two hours late for a movie screening. I took her into the ladies room, told her not to breathe, and sewed her into the dress.

When her lessons were over and Marilyn was about to return to Hollywood to film *Something's Got to Give*, we were invited to make omelets at her going-away party. Marilyn asked for hers plain, with no butter or oil, explaining that she had to watch her calories—even though she had a champagne glass in each hand!

"THE FIRST TIME I WALKED INTO SERENDIPITY, I WAS 17 AND I THOUGHT I HAD DIED AND GONE TO HEAVEN. I'D NEVER SEEN A PLACE OF SUCH WHIMSY BEFORE—OR SINCE, AS A MATTER OF FACT. WHEN IT CAME TO FROZEN BLENDED DRINKS, SERENDIPITY WAS DECADES AHEAD OF ITS TIME. THE FRRROZEN HOT CHOCOLATE IS STILL THE BEST DRINK OF ITS KIND."

— CANDICE BERGEN

MISS MILTON'S LOVELY FUDGE PIE

This is it, the decadent pie that seduced the seductive Marilyn Monroe. She simply couldn't get enough of it. Patch brought this recipe with him from Arkansas, where it was named for his sister Milton.

One alluring 8-inch pie for 6 or more

FOR THE PIE:

Unsalted butter for the pan

1/4 cup all-purpose flour

3 tablespoons cocoa

1 teaspoon baking powder

1/4 teaspoon salt

1/2 cup (1 stick) unsalted butter, cold

4 ounces (4 squares) bitter-sweet chocolate, chopped

3 large eggs

1 cup sugar

1 teaspoon vanilla extract

1/4 cup sour cream

Confectioners' sugar, to garnish

FOR THE COULIS:

1 pound fresh or frozen raspberries (if frozen, thaw completely)

1 tablespoon cornstarch

2 tablespoons sugar

• To make the pie: preheat your oven to 325 degrees. Butter an 8-inch round pie pan and line with parchment paper.

• Sift together the flour, cocoa, baking powder, and salt. In a double boiler over hot water, carefully melt the butter and chocolate, stirring to mix. In a large bowl, whisk the eggs, sugar, vanilla, and sour cream together. Add the melted chocolate and mix completely. Fold in the flour mixture and stir only until the batter is uniformly brown.

• Pour the batter into the prepared pan. Bake for 30 to 40 minutes, just until the batter is set and no longer jiggles when touched. Do not overbake; it should be moist and slightly gooey.

• While the pie bakes, make the coulis: puree the berries and pass through a sieve. (If you are using fresh berries, you may wish to reserve a few to use as a garnish when serving.) Mix the cornstarch with a little cold water until smooth. Place the berry puree, the cornstarch, and the sugar in a saucepan and heat to simmer. Cook 1 minute, then cool. Chill before using.

• After removing pie from oven, allow it to cool completely in the pan. Carefully turn it out of the pan, remove the parchment paper, and dust lightly with confectioners' sugar. Serve warm or room temperature with raspberry coulis.

"ONE OF MY GREATEST MEMORIES AS A CHILD WAS MY MOM, ON SPECIAL OCCASIONS, TAKING ME FOR FRRROZEN HOT CHOCOLATE. NOW I GET TO SHARE THAT SPECIAL TREAT WITH MY CHILDREN. I DON'T KNOW WHO WAS MORE EXCITED WHEN WE WENT THE FIRST TIME, ME OR MY DAUGHTER!"

— SARAH MICHELLE GELLER

MORE DELE

DELIG

DEFY

CTABLE

HTS THAT

CATEGORIZATION

ALMOND PEAR DELIGHT

Four peerless pears

4 firm pears, such as Bartlett

2 cups sugar

4 cups water

1 tablespoon lemon juice (about half a lemon)

5 whole cloves

1 cinnamon stick

2 ounces (4 teaspoons) slivered almonds

Whipped cream, page 56

• Peel the pears, leaving on the stems. Cut them in half from top to bottom, and core. Bring the sugar and water to a boil in a wide saucepan or small stock pot over high heat. Add the lemon juice, cloves, and cinnamon stick, and stir until the sugar is dissolved. Carefully add the pears, cut side down. Place a small lid or plate over the pears to keep them submerged. Cover the pot with a fitted lid, and boil for 5 minutes.

• Reduce the heat to a simmer, and continue cooking until the pears are soft but not mushy, about 30 minutes. Reserve the syrup.

• Meanwhile, toast the almonds in a skillet over medium heat, being careful not to burn them.

• Serve two pear halves hot, warm, or chilled, in a dessert dish, sprinkled with a teaspoonful of almonds and topped with a dollop of whipped cream. You may also, if you like, reduce the syrup by about half by simmering over medium heat, and spoon over pears when serving. Prepared pears may be refrigerated, with a bit of syrup, in a covered container for up to 3 days.

"WHEN I WAS EXPECTING OUR FIRST SON, MY HUSBAND AND I OFTEN STOPPED IN FOR A FRRROZEN HOT CHOCOLATE, WHICH I ADORED. SOON AFTER I WOULD FEEL LOTS OF ACTIVITY FROM THE BABY. HE MUST HAVE LOVED IT, TOO!"

— EVELYN LAUDER

BLUEBERRY BETTY

One bettiful loaf for 6 or more

3 cups bread cubes (1 large loaf), from a brioche or challah

1/2 cup melted butter, plus extra for the pan

4 cups fresh or frozen blueberries (if frozen, thaw completely and drain thoroughly)

1/2 cup brown sugar

2 tablespoons lemon juice

1/4 cup fine bread crumbs, made from fresh bread in a food processor

1/2 tablespoon unsalted butter, cold, cut into small pieces

Whipped cream, page 56

• Preheat your oven to 375 degrees. Mix the bread cubes and melted butter in a medium bowl, and spread one-third of the bread cubes evenly on the bottom of a well-buttered 9 x 5-inch loaf pan. Scatter one-third of the blueberries over this, then one-third of the sugar, spreading each evenly. Sprinkle one-third of the lemon juice over everything. Repeat this process two more times, using all of the bread cubes, blueberries, sugar, and lemon juice. Press down on the ingredients lightly to compress. Sprinkle the bread crumbs over the top, and dot with cold butter.

• Cover the pan in foil and bake it for 30 minutes. Remove the foil and bake Betty for another 15 minutes. Serve her warm with a dollop of whipped cream. Store wrapped in the refrigerator.

A JAUNT IN CAMELOT

The divine Jackie Kennedy visited us for the first time when she was a senator's wife, with John Jr. on the way. She fell in love with a gingham muumuu that I had designed, declared it the ultimate maternity dress, and ordered six in almost every color of the rainbow. That dress went on to hit the pages of *Vogue*, and Jackie became a lifelong customer.

When she was the first lady, she bought an antique wooden child's desk in our gift shop. She said that it was for John Jr., so that he would feel as if he were having a normal school experience even though he was being privately tutored in the White House. After her death, the desk was seen at an auction of her estate.

Jackie was known among the staff to be a gracious and humble customer, always willing to wait for a table if necessary and happy to sit anywhere. She often brought her young children. As they grew into teenagers, John came to meet his friends and Caroline to try on makeup in the gift shop. Years later, Jackie brought her grandchildren, eager to share Serendipity with the next generation.

CHERRY PAN DOWDY

About 8 frumpy cakes

FOR THE FILLING:

2 (15.5-ounce) cans pitted cherries

1/2 cup kirsch liqueur

1 tablespoon cornstarch

1/4 cup sugar

FOR THE BISCUITS:

2 cups all-purpose flour

4 teaspoons baking powder

2 tablespoons sugar

1/2 teaspoon salt

2 tablespoons unsalted butter, cold, cut into small pieces, plus extra for the pan

2/3 cup cold milk

1 large egg

1 tablespoon heavy cream

Granulated sugar for dusting

Whipped cream, page 56

• Drain the cherries well, reserving the juice. Macerate the cherries in the kirsch for 2 hours.

• To make the biscuits: preheat your oven to 425 degrees. Combine the flour, baking powder, sugar, and salt in the bowl of a food processor. Process briefly to blend; add the butter and process until the mixture resembles coarse meal, 15 to 30 seconds. Add the milk and process just until incorporated; the dough will be dry.

• Working the dough as little as possible, turn it out onto a clean surface and bring it together with your hands into a ball. Press the ball flat to a thickness of 1/2 inch. Cut out biscuits with a sharp 2 1/2-inch round cutter and place them on a buttered baking sheet, 1 inch apart.

• Lightly beat the egg in a small dish, add the cream, and stir. Brush each biscuit with the egg wash, and then sprinkle with granulated sugar. Bake for 10 minutes, until golden brown and puffed. Transfer to a rack. Keep warm for serving.

• To make the filling: drain the macerated cherries again, adding the kirsch to the reserved juice. Set the cherries aside.

• Blend 2 tablespoons of the cherry liquid with the cornstarch until there are no lumps. Combine the rest of the liquid with the sugar in a medium saucepan. Blend in the cornstarch mixture. Bring to a boil and cook for 2 minutes. Remove from heat.

• In another saucepan, heat the cherries with as much of the sauce as you desire. The more sauce, the more will soak into the biscuits.

• To serve, split a warm biscuit in half. Place 1/2 cup warm cherry sauce on bottom half of the biscuit. Place the other half biscuit on top, forming a sandwich. Slather the whole thing in whipped cream.

CHOCOLATE CRÊPES

About 20 luscious pancakes

5 large eggs

1 cup (scant) whole milk

1 tablespoon brandy

4 tablespoons (1/2 stick) unsalted butter, melted and cooled

1/2 cup chocolate syrup, such as Hershey's

1/3 cup all-purpose flour, sifted

Unsalted butter for the pan (and for serving, optional)

Sugar for serving (optional)

Ice cream (optional)

• In a large mixing bowl, whisk the eggs to break up. Add the milk, brandy, melted butter, and syrup, and stir. Whisk in the flour slowly, so no lumps form. Do not overmix; stop as soon as the flour is completely incorporated.

• In a crêpe pan or large nonstick skillet, melt 1 teaspoon of butter over medium-high heat. Have two clean plates ready. When butter bubbles, quickly pour in one ladle of crêpe batter (about 2 table-spoons) and roll the pan around so the entire bottom is covered in a very thin layer. Cook the crêpe, shaking once or twice to prevent sticking, until most but not all of the batter on top has set, or the bottom is golden brown, about 2 to 3 minutes.

• Slide the crêpe onto a plate, cooked side down. Quickly invert the plate into the pan, flipping the crêpe. Cook another 1 to 2 minutes, until golden brown. Slide onto the second plate to cool.

• Continue with remaining batter, adding more butter as necessary, stacking the crêpes on top of each other on the second plate. Serve warm or room temperature, with butter and sugar or ice cream, or as an Ice Cream Crêpe Sundae, page 122.

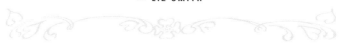

"TAKING KIDS TO SERENDIPITY IS ALWAYS SUREFIRE.
BETWEEN THE HOT DOGS AND THE FABULOUS SUNDAES,
THEY CAN GET UP AND SHOP. ALWAYS FUN TO RUN ACROSS
A MOVIE STAR OR TWO DOING THE SAME THING!"

— LIZ SMITH

FTATATEETA'S TOAST

With a name like that, it's no wonder the waiters call this dish Fat's Toast for short. But in case you're wondering where that tongue-twisting moniker comes from, Ftatateeta (pronounced fa-tah-ta-tee-tah) was Cleopatra's handmaiden in George Bernard Shaw's *Caesar and Cleopatra*. Ever the clever wordsmith, our cofounder Patch thought a mouthful of a name would do justice to this mouthful of a dish.

Four ftantastic sandwiches

Pinch of ground cinnamon

Pinch of ground nutmeg

Pinch of finely grated orange zest

1 tablespoon brandy

2/3 cup milk

2 large eggs

8 slices white bread, the crusts trimmed to form a uniform edge

Unsalted butter for cooking

2 (8-ounce) packages cream cheese

Jam of your choice, preferably rhubarb-ginger

• Combine the cinnamon, nutmeg, orange zest, and brandy in a mixing bowl and stir with a wire whisk. Add milk and continue whisking until blended. In a separate bowl, whisk the eggs until frothy; add them to the spice mixture and blend well.

• Dip all 8 slices of bread in this mixture and brown them on one side on a hot, well-buttered griddle. Flip half of the slices and top them with nice, thick slices of cream cheese. Cover the cream cheese with remaining 4 slices of bread, browned side down. Flip again to brown top sides.

• Cut each sandwich in half on the diagonal; top with a dollop of jam.

"BELOVED LANDMARKS OF OUR CHILDHOOD DISAPPEAR, QUALITY DISSIPATES, AND THINGS THAT ONCE SEEMED ENORMOUS APPEAR TO SHRINK. NOT SERENDIPITY. AFTER ALL THESE YEARS, SERENDIPITY IS BETTER THAN EVER."

—DANIELLE STEEL

CANDIDE'S APPLES

Six optimistic apples

6 small apples

6 wooden skewers or Popsicle sticks

1 cup unsulphured molasses

1 cup sugar

1 teaspoon cider vinegar

1/3 teaspoon salt

1/4 cup water

2 tablespoons unsalted butter, softened

• Prepare the apples for dipping by removing their stems and inserting a wooden skewer or Popsicle stick into the top of each one. Have a cooling rack ready by the stove, set over a tray to catch any drippings.

• Combine the molasses, sugar, vinegar, salt, and water in a medium saucepan. Cook slowly over medium heat, stirring occasionally, until the mixture reaches 270 degrees on a candy thermometer, or when a small quantity dropped into cold water forms a hard ball. Remove from the heat and stir in the butter. Immediately dip the apples one by one into the syrup, covering the entire surface. Place on the rack to cool. If the syrup begins to harden before all the apples have been coated, reheat slightly and continue. Cool apples completely.

"I WAS VISITING NEW YORK CITY, WHEN, AS PERFECT TIMING WOULD HAVE IT, I WAS RUSHED TO THE DENTIST FOR EMERGENCY ORAL SURGERY. I WALKED OUT A COUPLE HOURS LATER WITH A SWOLLEN MOUTH AND AN ORDER TO REST AND RELAX. I WAS STARVING—THEN SERENDIPITY CAME TO MIND. I'M SURE MY RASPBERRY-TOPPED CHOCOLATE SUNDAE WAS EXACTLY WHAT THE DENTIST MEANT WHEN HE SAID, 'GO BACK TO THE HOTEL AND TAKE A NICE LONG NAP.'"

—TORI AMOS

CHOCOLATE CHIP PIZZA

Two plump 12-inch pizzas

2 1/2 cups all-purpose flour

1 teaspoon baking soda

1 teaspoon salt

2 sticks unsalted butter, softened, plus extra for pan

3/4 cup sugar

3/4 cup packed brown sugar

2 large eggs

1 teaspoon vanilla extract

1 (12-ounce) package chocolate chips

1 cup chopped nuts

• Preheat your oven to 375 degrees. Sift together the flour, baking soda, and salt; set aside. With a mixer, cream together the butter and sugars. Beat in the eggs and vanilla, then gradually add the flour mixture and stir just until smooth. Fold in the chocolate chips and nuts. Use whatever kind of nuts—or a combination—that strikes your fancy.

• Spread half of the batter in a buttered 12-inch deep-dish pizza pan and bake for 20 to 25 minutes, until a cake tester inserted in the center comes out clean. Once cool, remove pizza from pan and set aside. Re-butter the pan, fill with remaining half of mixture, and bake as above. Serve each pizza in wedges, with whipped cream and chocolate syrup for a fancy look. Store, without any topping, tightly wrapped at room temperature.

"THE FIRST TIME I WENT TO SERENDIPITY I WAS NINE MONTHS OLD, SO I AM TOLD. I USED TO LOVE GOING THERE AND GETTING THOSE BIG FROZEN CHOCOLATE ICE CREAMY FLOATY DRINKS! NOW I HAVE THREE CHILDREN OF MY OWN AND HAVE CONTINUED THE RITUAL WITH THEM. I CAN HONESTLY SAY I HAVE ENJOYED AND LOVED SERENDIPITY FOR 45 YEARS!"

—MELANIE GRIFFITH

"WHEN MY DAUGHTER MOVED BACK TO NEW YORK, ONE OF THE FIRST PLACES WE WENT WAS SERENDIPITY. IT HAS NEVER BEEN BY ACCIDENT THAT I HAVE RETURNED, TIME AND TIME AGAIN."

—TIPPI HEDREN

MOONSHINE APPLE FRITTERS

Eight potent fritters

1 large egg

1 tablespoon sugar

1 teaspoon salt

2/3 cup all-purpose flour (or enough to make a heavy batter)

1 teaspoon baking powder

1 cup milk

1 tablespoon white or dark rum

4 to 6 apples, peeled and cored

Shortening for frying

Confectioners' sugar for garnish

• In a medium bowl, beat the egg with a wire whisk and blend in the sugar and salt. Sift together the flour and baking powder, and add them to the egg mixture alternately with the milk. Mix thoroughly to make a smooth, thick batter, blending in the rum as you whisk.

• Cut each apple in 4 or more rings; dip the rings in the batter to coat them completely. Yields 16 to 30 depending on apple size and size of slices (rings).

• Heat shortening at least 1-inch deep in a heavy cast-iron skillet. Fry the dipped apple slices until the batter turns golden brown on one side, then flip and fry golden brown on the other side.

• Drain the fritters on paper towels, sprinkle with confectioners' sugar, and enjoy.

"I HAVE SPENT MANY BIRTHDAYS AT SERENDIPITY FROM THE AGE OF SEVEN ON UP. WE USED TO HAVE CONTESTS TO SEE WHO COULD DRINK A FRRROZEN HOT CHOCOLATE THE FASTEST. THE ONLY 'BRAIN FREEZE' HEADACHE I ENJOY COMES FROM THAT TREAT! I CAN'T WAIT FOR MY BABY TO BE A CUSTOMER."

— BROOKE SHIELDS

THE NEW AGE RAGE

The success of Serendipity may well have been written in the stars. The restaurant had a fortuitous "birth," according to our current official astrologer, Shelley Ackerman. We first opened the doors on September 15, 1954, which makes Serendipity a Virgo with Aquarius rising. "That means it's hardworking with a flair for the unconventional. Put those aspects together and Serendipity was bound to be a smashing triumph," reports Ackerman. The proud parents—or three proud princes—were in harmony with the stars as well. Ackerman performed a full reading of the three owners' astrological charts. "Calvin and Patch were both Cancers, and Cancers love to prepare and serve food. Stephen is a Capricorn, a sign that comes with loads of style, ambition, and fine taste."

When we moved the restaurant, our trusty soothsayer at that time, Ursule Molinero, determined that we were in harmonious vibration with the new location, and our mystical disposition has continued to serve us well. It has required strict adherence to our astrological destiny, however. Calvin refused to hire any employees whose stars weren't compatible with ours. Sylvester Stallone applied for a waiter's job in the early seventies but was turned down because his sign didn't jive with ours. No matter, he hit it big a few years later.

When we're not studying stars, we try to keep in touch with old friends—from time to time we've held séances to make contact with the spirits of the customers we miss most. At one session, Marilyn Monroe confided that her one true love had been her mother. At another, the psychic John Edwards received a message from Andy Warhol telling us to be careful of the skylights. We didn't pay that tidbit much heed until a month later—a large tree branch fell through a skylight into our kitchen!

THICK,
AND
PUDDIN

RICH, DREAMY GS

COCONUT CREAM PUDDING

Eight creamy cups

7 teaspoons (2 envelopes plus 1 teaspoon) unflavored powdered gelatin

1/2 cup milk, cold

4 large egg whites, room temperature

1/2 teaspoon salt

3/4 cup confectioners' sugar

3 cups heavy cream, cold

5 teaspoons vanilla extract

3 cups flaked, sweetened coconut

• Combine the gelatin with the milk and heat it in the microwave, in 10-second bursts, until the gelatin dissolves. Do not boil. The mixture will appear a bit curdled as the milk solids separate due to the heat. Allow it to cool a bit, but not so much that it re-solidifies.

• In a clean medium bowl with clean beaters, beat the egg whites with the salt. Slowly add 6 tablespoons of the confectioners' sugar and whip until stiff, glossy peaks form.

• In a large bowl, beat the cream and vanilla with the remaining confectioners' sugar just until stiff peaks form. Fold the egg whites into the whipped cream. Don't overmix—it's okay to stop when there are still some streaks. Add the gelatin and fold just until incorporated. Fold in 2 1/2 cups of the coconut.

• Spoon the mixture into eight 1-cup ramekins. (If you have fresh coconut shells, use them in place of the ramekins.) Cover each ramekin with plastic wrap, and then chill until completely set, at least 2 hours. Toast the remaining 1/2 cup coconut in a wide skillet over low heat, stirring occasionally. Top each pudding with a tablespoon of coconut. Serve chilled. Please see note (page 69) about using raw egg whites.

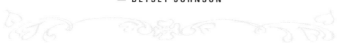

"I ALWAYS USED TO TAKE MY DAUGHTER LULU TO SERENDIPITY, WHEN SHE WAS LITTLE. SHE WAS IN HEAVEN THERE—WITH THE FRRROZEN HOT CHOCOLATE, THE TOYS, THE COLORS, THE DECOR."

— BETSEY JOHNSON

CRÈME BRÛLÉE JULIA

One surprising 9-inch
pudding for 6 or more

1 pint fresh raspberries

3 large eggs

3 large egg yolks

1/4 cup sugar

1 1/3 cups heavy cream

2/3 cup milk

1 teaspoon vanilla extract

3/4 cup superfine sugar

• Preheat your oven to 300 degrees. Arrange the raspberries in a single layer at the bottom of a 9-inch round baking dish. In medium mixing bowl, beat the eggs and yolks together with the sugar. In a heavy saucepan bring the cream, milk, and vanilla to a boil over medium heat. Pour the mixture very slowly into the eggs, whisking constantly. Return mixture to the saucepan. Cook over moderate heat, stirring constantly, until the custard coats the back of the spoon (about 4 minutes). Remove from heat.

• Carefully pour the custard through a sieve over the raspberries in the prepared baking dish. Place a large pan in the middle rack of your oven. Place the baking dish in the center of the pan. Fill the pan with hot water halfway up the side of the dish. Bake for 30 to 40 minutes, just until center of custard is no longer wet.

• Remove the baked custard from the water bath and allow it to cool to room temperature. Place a piece of plastic wrap right on the surface of the custard and chill completely.

• Immediately before serving, preheat the broiler. Sift the superfine sugar evenly over the top of the custard, spreading it to the edges. Set the custard as close to the heat as possible. Broil until browned but not burned, about 1 1/2 minutes. Watch closely. Scoop dollops to serve. Wrap tightly and store in the refrigerator.

"SERENDIPITY IS WHERE YOU GO TO FEEL LIKE A KID AGAIN."

—ALEC BALDWIN

RICE DREAM WITH PINEAPPLE SAUCE

5 unreal cups

FOR THE PUDDING:

Salt

2/3 cup uncooked white rice

1 1/2 teaspoons
(1/2 envelope) unflavored
powdered gelatin

2 tablespoons milk

1 large egg white,
room temperature

2 tablespoons plus 2 tea-
spoons confectioners' sugar

10 tablespoons heavy cream

2 tablespoons whole milk

1 teaspoon vanilla extract

FOR THE SAUCE:

1 cup sugar

1 1/4 cup (one 15-ounce can,
drained) crushed pineapple

• Cook rice for 25 to 30 minutes in salted, boiling water until very soft. Drain it and rinse with cold water; drain again thoroughly.

• Combine the gelatin and milk in a small bowl and set that bowl into a bath of hot water. When the gelatin has dissolved, remove from hot water and let cool.

• Beat the egg white with a pinch of salt until frothy, adding the sugar gradually while beating, then whip to stiffen. In a separate bowl, beat the heavy cream and milk until it has the consistency of thin whipped cream. Add the cream to the egg white mixture. Add the gelatin and fold in the rice and vanilla. Pour the pudding into custard cups and chill. Please see note about eating raw egg whites, page 69.

• To make the sauce, combine the sugar with 1 cup of water in a saucepan, stirring over low heat until dissolved. Measure out 3/4 cup of this syrup and combine with pineapple. Drown the pudding with the sauce and garnish with a large slice of fresh pineapple if you have it.

"THROUGH THE YEARS, SERENDIPITY HAS BEEN
A NEIGHBORHOOD HAVEN WHERE I TRULY ENJOY SHARING
A SPECIAL DAY OF LUNCH AND DESSERT WITH MY FRIENDS
AND ESPECIALLY MY GRANDDAUGHTERS."

—MATILDA RAFFA CUOMO

DARK DEVIL CHOCOLATE MOUSSE

Six to 8 devilish servings

4 large eggs, separated, room temperature

1 tablespoon vanilla extract

2 tablespoons brandy

12 ounces unsweetened chocolate, melted and cooled

1 1/2 cups heavy cream

1/4 cup sugar

• Whisk the egg yolks, vanilla, and brandy together in the top half of a double boiler over simmering water. Cook, continuing to whisk vigorously, until the mixture is thick and hot to the touch, 7 to 10 minutes.

• Add the yolk mixture to the chocolate in three additions, folding carefully between each. The chocolate will thicken considerably.

• In a clean medium bowl using a mixer, with clean beaters, whip the cream until soft peaks form. Carefully fold the cream into the chocolate mixture in three additions, stopping while there are still some white streaks.

• In a second clean mixing bowl, with clean beaters, whip the egg whites until frothy. While continuing to beat, add the sugar in a slow stream. Whip until soft peaks form. Carefully fold the whites into the chocolate in three additions, stopping just when the mousse is a uniform color and no streaks remain. Please see note about eating raw egg whites, page 69.

• Spoon the mousse into 6 to 8 pretty dessert glasses. Cover in plastic wrap and refrigerate at least 30 minutes. Serve cold., with a dollop of whipped cream if you like. Use any extra mousse to make the mountainous Cheesecake Vesuvius Sundae, page 123.

"WHAT'S MY FAVORITE SERENDIPITY MEMORY? WATCHING MY SON DRINK HIS FIRST FRRROZEN HOT CHOCOLATE."

— CALISTA FLOCKHART

SMOOTH,

IRRESIS

FROZEN

ICY, AND TIBLE DRINKS

SERENDIPITY'S BEST-KEPT SECRET:
FRRROZEN
HOT CHOCOLATE

It's famous, it's infamous, it's notorious. It has destroyed diets and led to love affairs. Marriages have been proposed over it, couples have been wed in it, princes have been made from it. People have traveled from all corners of the world for just one sip of our creamy, dreamy, icy blend of chocolatey goodness. It'll make you want to blow bubbles through your straw. It makes everyone a child again.

For years, fans begged and pleaded and offered their firstborn for the recipe, but we three princes guarded the formula with our lives. It was such a closely kept secret that not even the White House could gain access to it. Jackie Kennedy once requested the recipe so that it could be served at a gala evening at the White House. I offered to travel to Washington to make it myself, but when my security clearance didn't come through in time, I refused to hand over the secret formula—not even to the first lady herself!

When customers asked how it was made, we would respond that we had a Rube Goldberg machine churning it out in the back—a hodgepodge of arms, wheels, gears, handles, paddles, and even canaries in cages working in concert to concoct the magic elixir. We would never let on that it was as simple as a blender and some magnificent chocolate.

And now, to thank our customers for fifty great years, we've finally decided to share the secret recipe with the world. For truly authentic Serendipity taste, throw a sprinkle of magic in the mix. For this and all the frozen drinks that follow, the recipe yields one gigantic Serendipity-sized serving, which is perfect for sharing. Enjoy.

6 half-ounce pieces of a variety of your favorite chocolates

2 teaspoons storebought hot chocolate mix

1 1/2 tablespoons sugar

1 1/2 cups milk

3 cups ice

Whipped cream, page 56

Chocolate shavings

• Chop the chocolate into small pieces and place it in the top of a double boiler over simmering water, stirring occasionally until melted. Add the hot chocolate mix and sugar, stirring constantly until thoroughly blended. Remove from heat and slowly add 1/2 cup of the milk and stir until smooth. Cool to room temperature.

• In a blender place the remaining cup of milk, the room temperature chocolate mixture, and the ice. Blend on high speed until smooth and the consistency of a frozen daiquiri. Pour into a giant goblet and top with whipped cream and chocolate shavings. Enjoy with a spoon or a straw—or both!

FRRROZEN
HAUTE CHOCOLATE

PRICE: $25,000*

6 sheets 23K edible gold leaf

18K gold bracelet with 1 carat pure white diamonds (Euphoria New York)

Serendipity's secret cocoa blend (includes 14 cocoas)

14 additional expensive, exotic, and rare cocoas (Fauchon, Charbonnel et Walker, Schokinag, and Droste, among others)

1 cup whole milk

3 cups ice

5 grams 23K edible gold flakes, plus extra for sprinkling

Whipped cream, page 56

La Madeline au Truffle (the world's most expensive chocolate truffle); broken into pieces

• Line a goblet with the gold leaf; pieces of gold leaf should overhang the goblet perimeter. Place diamond bracelet around goblet.

• Add the secret cocoa blend to a medium bowl and whisk with the additional cocoas. Whisk the 5 grams of 23K edible gold with the cocoas. Heat the milk in a small saucepan just until hot. Add the cocoas and whisk to combine. Cool to room temperature.

• In a blender place the room temperature cocoa-milk mixture and the ice. Blend on high speed until smooth and the consistency of a frozen daiquiri. Add gold flakes. Pour into the prepared goblet and top with whipped cream and the chocolate truffle pieces. Enjoy with an 18K gold 98-gram spoon encrusted with 3 carats of black, white, and chocolate diamonds from Euphoria New York jewelers.

*The profits of this Guinness World Record Dessert go to charity.

PARADISE FOR KIDS OF ALL AGES

Children fidget at other restaurants, but not at Serendipity. Kids can be kids here, and adults can be kids, too. Steven Spielberg taught yo-yo tricks to his son (without breaking any valuables!). Dustin Hoffman, his wife Anne, and their daughter came in once for a bite—all of them on roller skates.

Lots of celebs have hosted their kids' birthday parties here, including Michael Douglas, Francis Ford Coppola, and Candice Bergen. A birthday wish came true for one special child when Arnold Schwarzenegger met with him at the restaurant, as part of the Make-a-Wish Foundation. Robin Williams kept an 11-year-old girl with leukemia laughing for two hours over dinner and dessert. Ron Howard even had a double birthday party for his daughter and himself, complete with two cakes!

FRRROZEN WHITE HOT CHOCOLATE

6 ounces white chocolate

3/4 cup milk

6 fresh mint leaves, plus 1 or 2 sprigs for garnish

2 cups ice

Whipped cream, page 56

Maraschino cherries, candy canes, or dark chocolate sprinkles, optional

• Place the chocolate, broken into small pieces, in a heavy saucepan over very low heat and stir until melted. Remove from heat and whisk in half the milk until well blended. Place the remaining milk in a blender with chocolate mixture, mint leaves, and ice. Blend at high speed until smooth and frothy, and the ice is pulverized. Pour into chilled goblets, top with whipped cream, mint sprigs, and optional cherries, candy canes, or sprinkles.

PEANUT BUTTER FRRROZEN HOT CHOCOLATE

Follow the instructions for Frrrozen Hot Chocolate, adding 2 tablespoons of peanut butter or peanut butter topping to the blender.

FRRROZEN MOCHACCINO

We put this drink on the menu in the mid-sixties, a mere thirty years before Starbucks rolled out their version in 1995. When Julia Roberts visited us with then-beau Benjamin Bratt, she ordered Frrrozen Mochaccino—but the superstar handed the waiter a package of soy milk, sweetly requesting that her dessert be dairy-free.

To make, follow instructions for Frrrozen Hot Chocolate, adding a shot of espresso to the blender.

SALTED CARAMEL FRRROZEN HOT CHOCOLATE

6 half-ounce pieces
of a variety of your
favorite chocolates

2 teaspoons storebought
hot chocolate mix

1 1/2 tablespoons sugar

1 1/2 cups milk

2/3 cup caramel sauce

1/2 teaspoon fleur de sel,
plus extra for sprinkling

3 cups ice

Whipped cream, page 56

• Chop the chocolate into small pieces and place it in the top of a double boiler over simmering water, stirring occasionally until melted. Add the hot chocolate mix and sugar, stirring constantly until thoroughly blended. Remove from the heat and slowly add ½ cup of the milk and stir until smooth. Cool to room temperature.

• In a blender place the remaining cup of milk, the room temperature chocolate mixture, all but 4 tablespoons of the caramel sauce, the fleur de sel, and the ice. Blend on high speed until smooth and the consistency of a frozen daiquiri. Pour into a giant goblet and top with whipped cream. Drizzle the remaining 4 tablespoons caramel sauce on the whipped cream and around the edge of the goblet. Sprinkle with fleur de sel.

A MATTER OF PRIDE

In the early sixties, Bette Davis once came into the restaurant for a business meeting with her manager. When they had finished she asked for the bill. Her waiter, a sweet fellow who was a great fan, told her not to worry, that he would be honored to take care of it. She arched her eyebrows in a characteristic turn and announced curtly, "I never let a man pay a check for me. Call the owner over." Trying to cover up my flustered nerves, I walked to her table and steadied myself for an earful. She preached in her smoky drawl, loud enough for the entire restaurant to hear: "I'm from New England. I do things my own way. I make my own movies. And, I pay my own bills." "Of course, Miss Davis, you'll have a check right away," I said as I whisked away like a messenger from the Virgin Queen's throne. We all came away that day with even more admiration for the grand dame. Miss Davis was no Jezebel, but a self-made woman indebted to no man.

PINK ICE

Gloria Vanderbilt was the inspiration for this frosty drink. During the fifties she was notorious for her love of the color pink, and would come in to the restaurant dressed entirely in her favorite rosy hue, with icy-white makeup. She once commissioned fifty miniature pink topiaries in porcelain pots, which I stayed up all night to finish. Ms. Vanderbilt's son always enjoyed ordering his mom's signature drink.

1 1/2 lemons, peel and pith removed, seeded

1 tablespoon sugar

Dash of red food coloring

1 cup water

• Cut the lemon into chunks and combine it with the sugar, coloring, and water in a blender half-full of ice. After blending at high speed, add more ice if the drink is slushy. If it's too thick, add more liquid.

• Top with a lemon slice.

"STEPPING INTO SERENDIPITY IS LIKE ENTERING THE INSIDE OF A CAKE. I FEEL LIKE IT HAS ALWAYS BEEN A PART OF MY FAMILY, A PLACE OF JOY, AND SUCH WONDERFUL MEMORIES. IT'S ONE OF THOSE PLACES THAT MAKES NEW YORK THE REMARKABLE CITY THAT IT IS."

— GLORIA VANDERBILT

"I'LL NEVER FORGET WHEN I WAS ABOUT 8 YEARS OLD MY BIRTHDAY PRESENT WAS A MEAL AT SERENDIPITY WITH MY BEST FRIEND, ALL ON OUR OWN. NOW, I STILL GO WITH MY FRIENDS, AND WHEN I HAVE KIDS, IT WILL BE THE FIRST PLACE I TAKE THEM."

— ANDERSON COOPER

MORE FRRROZEN DRINKS...

For each of the recipes below, combine the ingredients listed in a blender half-full of ice. After blending at high speed, add more ice if the drink is slushy. If it's too thick, add more liquid. "Coconut snow" is shredded sweetened coconut that you've ground fine in your food processor.

FRRROZEN PINEAPPLE LIME

1 cup pineapple juice

5 pineapple chunks, fresh or canned

1 tablespoon applesauce

1 tablespoon Rose's Lime Juice

• Top with whipped cream and green sugar.

FRRROZEN ESPRESSO

1 cup espresso, room temperature

1 teaspoon instant espresso powder

1 teaspoon sugar

• Top with whipped cream and grated chocolate or lemon peel and a coffee bean.

APRICOT SMUSH

1 cup stewed apricots, room temperature

1 cup apricot nectar

• Top with whipped cream and an apricot, or whipped cream, confetti-colored nonpareils, and a cherry.

NOVEMBER 1959

1 cup cranberry juice

Generous pinch shredded coconut

1 tablespoon coconut snow

1 tablespoon whipped cream

• Top with whipped cream and red sugar.

OREO EXPRESS

4 Oreo cookies, crushed

1 1/2 cups milk

2 scoops of ice cream, your favorite flavor

• Top with whipped cream and a whole Oreo.

NEW YORK'S

OUTRA

SUND

MOST
GEOUS
AES

HOW TO MAKE A SERENDIPITOUS SUNDAE

At Serendipity we have a simple philosophy about sundaes: the bigger and more outrageous, the better! We make ours in a giant goblet, but your favorite bowl will work just as well. We start by coating the goblet with a nice, thick layer of sauce. Then we plop in some very voluptuous scoops of ice cream, followed by another drenching of sauce, a dousing of toppings, and, of course, whipped cream. For a classic hot fudge sundae, use hot fudge sauce and vanilla ice cream. Each of these recipes makes one sundae—but it's all right if you share.

FORBIDDEN BROADWAY SUNDAE

Theater East, a small theater that once was on Serendipity's street, put on a play every year called *Forbidden Broadway*, lampooning the current Broadway shows. We named this sundae for their wacky productions.

Hot fudge

1 generous hunk of Chocolate Blackout Cake, page 34

1 ample scoop of vanilla ice cream

Whipped cream, page 56

Chocolate shavings

Maraschino cherry

"I MET CALVIN 50 YEARS AGO WHEN HE WORKED BEHIND THE COUNTER AT HOWARD JOHNSON'S IN TIMES SQUARE. HE TOLD ME ABOUT OPENING A NEW BUSINESS AS I ENJOYED MY BUTTER BRICKLE SODA. WHEN SERENDIPITY FIRST OPENED, CALVIN TOOK TWO DOORS FROM HIS APARTMENT AND USED THEM AS TABLE TOPS. I LOVED MY HOT FUDGE SUNDAE AND ATE IT AT THE DOORS!"

— SHIRLEY MACLAINE

STRAWBERRY FIELDS SUNDAE

John Lennon was a devoted fan of Serendipity, so we named this one after his memorial, Strawberry Fields, which is located just blocks away from Serendipity in Central Park. When he and Yoko came to eat at the restaurant, they would have walked across this part of Central Park from their home on the Upper West Side.

1 slice of Crème de la Crème Cheesecake, page 37

1 momentous scoop of strawberry ice cream

Strawberry topping

Whipped cream, page 56

Fresh strawberries for garnish

500 SCOOPS, PLEASE!

In one particularly harried scene in the movie *One Fine Day*, Michelle Pfieffer visits Serendipity and gets a chocolate sundae dumped all over her. Only in Hollywood can a spilled sundae become so complicated. Pfieffer didn't want to film in New York away from her children, so the entire restaurant was recreated in a Los Angeles studio. I went there to serve as a technical advisor, ensuring that the restaurant—and the food!—were accurately depicted. Five hundred balls of chocolate ice cream were prepped and waiting in the freezer for the many necessary shots. Twelve takes later, it was a wrap. There was an awful lot of leftover chocolate ice cream.

GOLDEN OPULENCE SUNDAE

PRICE: $1,000

1 Baccarat Harcourt crystal goblet

5 scoops Tahitian vanilla bean ice cream wrapped in edible gold leaf

7 ounces Amedei Porcelana and Chuao chocolate

12 gold-leaf almonds

1 tablespoon exotic candied fruit

Gilded sugar flower for garnish

1 square Chuao chocolate

Knipschildt chocolate truffles

1 tablespoon Grande Passion caviar with passion fruit, blood orange, and Armagnac

1 mother-of-pearl caviar spoon

1 24-carat gold spoon

• In Baccarat crystal goblet, carefully place scoops of Tahitian vanilla ice cream wrapped in edible gold leaf.

• Cover in Amedei Porcelana and Chuao chocolate sauce.

• Decorate with gold-leaf almonds, candied fruit, sugar flower, and the square of Chuao chocolate.

• Place goblet on a gold leaf–lined saucer and decorate plate with gold-leaf almonds, chocolate truffles, passion fruit caviar with mother-of-pearl spoon, and a 24-carat gold spoon.

HATS AND DRESSES À LA MODE

I've always had a passion for fashion, and from our early days I was designing hats, dresses, and denim clothing, and selling them in the gift shop. I dyed fabrics on the roof of our building, and cut and sewed garments in a workroom above the restaurant. The well-heeled came to Serendipity for dessert and left with dresses and hats—and before long I was thrilled to have some true trendsetters wearing my designs.

A very young Brooke Shields modeled my hats after she made headlines in her first big film, *Pretty Baby*, in 1978. Catherine Deneuve once requested that a particular hat be sent to her in Paris to wear for the Yves Saint Laurent fashion show that night! She had reserved a seat for it on the Concorde, and she had it just in time for the show.

As a young designer I was thrilled when our celebrity customers wore my clothing. Cher purchased denim miniskirts from my collection. Jackie Kennedy asked me to make her a hostess pajama ensemble, which was at the height of fashion in the seventies. She picked out an apricot silk and a design with bell legs and sleeves, and lace trim. For Katharine Hepburn I designed a denim caftan with a large V-neck—she insisted on wearing a turtleneck underneath it to conceal any signs of aging.

TITANIC SUNDAE

When the musical *Titanic* opened on Broadway in 1997, we created this sundae in its honor. It's Titanic in form, and more important, it's Titanic in size!

3 scoops vanilla ice cream

Marshmallow fluff

Walnut topping

6 mini Oreo cookies

3 chocolate-dipped rolled
wafer cookies

Whipped cream, page 56,
tinted with blue food coloring

6 large marshmallows

• To create this majestic sundae, start with a banana split dish propped up on one end with a small cup or other small dish. Place this on a larger plate and fill the banana split dish with vanilla ice cream, Marshmallow fluff, and walnut topping to make your sinking ship. Place 3 mini Oreo cookies on each side to make portholes, and place chocolate-dipped wafer cookies in the center to make smoke stacks. Surround the boat with an ocean of blue whipped cream. To make the iceberg, stack the marshmallows on the plate and cover them with fluff.

ICE CREAM
CRÊPE SUNDAE

1 scoop vanilla ice cream

1 Chocolate Crêpe, page 82

Raspberry topping

• Wrap the ice cream in the crêpe and top with raspberry sauce.

YU DU FUN DU

Variety of fresh fruit (apples,
strawberries, cantaloupe,
banana, etc.)

Hot fudge

• Slice the fruit into bite-sized pieces and arrange on a plate around a bowl of hot fudge. Dip with forks or skewers. Fondu-licious!

SAND TART SUNDAE

Hot fudge

2 Aunt Buba's Sand Tarts, page 45

2 nice scoops of coffee ice cream

Whipped cream, page 56

CHEESECAKE VESUVIUS SUNDAE

Aptly named after Mt. Vesuvius in Italy, this sundae is nearly as large.

1 slice Crème de la Crème Cheesecake, page 37

1 serving Dark Devil Chocolate Mousse, page 99

Whipped cream, page 56

1/2 cup fresh strawberries, halved

Sliced almonds

1 cup hot fudge

• On a large plate, slice the cheesecake in two lengthwise and place the mousse in between the two halves. Cover the entire surface of the cake and plate in whipped cream, with a taller ring of whipped cream going around the edge of the plate. Sprinkle the strawberries and almonds over the whipped cream, then pour the hot fudge into the opening in the middle.

CINNAMON FUN SUNDAE

1 slice of Big Apple Pie, page 63

1 hulking scoop of cinnamon ice cream rolled in cinnamon sugar

Caramel topping

Whipped cream, page 56

Ground cinnamon to dust on top

1 cinnamon stick for garnish

OUTRAGEOUS BANANA SPLIT

2 bananas

5 whopping scoops of your favorite flavors of ice cream

5 toppings, whatever you like best. We suggest hot fudge, strawberry, pineapple, caramel, maple walnut, raspberry, butterscotch, or peanut butter

Whipped cream, page 56

Maraschino cherry

• Stick the bananas in the top so that they look like horns poking out. Trust us, it tastes better that way!

• To make a Coward's Portion Banana Split, use just 1 banana, 3 large scoops of ice cream, 3 toppings, and whipped cream.

"ROBYN BYRD COULD HAVE SERVED THE BANANA SPLITS ON HER SHOW, THEY'RE SO OBSCENE LOOKING."
—BOB SCHAEFFER

CAN'T SAY NO SUNDAE

Hot fudge

1 slice of Humble Pie, page 57

1 proud scoop of vanilla ice cream

Whipped cream, page 56

INDEX

CREDITS

Brett Bara wrote the book's text with Stephen Bruce. She is a New York–based writer, designer, and confectionary enthusiast. She has edited and written for a number of magazines, including *Marie Claire*, *Details*, *Men's Health*, and *Mademoiselle*.

Urbano Lora was born in the Dominican Republic and began working at Serendipity 3 at the age of seventeen as a baker's intern. Today he is Serendipity's master baker and ensures the quality and consistency of all the desserts that have made the restaurant famous.

Liz Steger, who is responsible for all of the photographs in the book, specializes in food and restaurant photography in New York City. She has photographed edibles and eateries for *Food Arts Magazine*, *New York* magazine, Ciao Bello Gelato, and the Waldorf-Astoria.

This revised edition first published in the United States of America in 2014 by

UNIVERSE PUBLISHING

A Division of Rizzoli International Publications, Inc.

300 Park Avenue South

New York, NY 10010

www.rizzoliusa.com

First published in the United States of America in 2004

Project Supervisor, Serendipity: Joseph Calderone

Project Manager, Serendipity: Joann Lee

Editor: Chris Steighner

Designer: Paul Kepple, Headcase Design

Additional Design: Kayleigh Jankowski

2014 2015 2016 2017 / 10 9 8 7 6 5 4 3 2 1

Printed in China

ISBN-13: 978-0-7893-2757-4

A MAP OF THE STARS

(SOME OF OUR FAVORITE
CUSTOMERS' FAVORITE SPOTS)

UPSTAIRS

JOHN
CUSACK

KATE
BECKINSALE

JACK
NICHOLSON

TYRA BANKS

JOHN LENNON

YOKO ONO

MOLLY
RINGWALD

JACLYN
SMITH

JACQUELINE
KENNEDY
ONASSIS

CAROLINE
KENNEDY

MICHAEL
DOUGLAS

FRANCESCO
SCAVULLO

DANNY
DEVITO

RHEA
PERLMAN

KIM
BASINGER